D0875865

VOLTAIRE

Voltaire

H. N. BRAILSFORD

LONDON
OXFORD UNIVERSITY PRESS
NEW YORK   TORONTO
1963

Oxford University Press, Amen House, London E.C.4

GLASGOW NEW YORK TORONTO MELBOURNE WELLINGTON
BOMBAY CALCUTTA MADRAS KARACHI LAHORE DACCA
CAPE TOWN SALISBURY NAIROBI IBADAN ACCRA
KUALA LUMPUR HONG KONG

First published in 1935 *and reprinted in* 1945 *and* 1947
First issued in OXFORD PAPERBACKS 1963

Printed in Great Britain

CONTENTS

I. Cradle to Bastille 7

II. Exile in England 22

III. Hermit and Courtier 33

IV. Liberal History 47

V. The Match with Frederick 75

VI. *Candide* 82

VII. He Cultivates his Garden 94

VIII. The Calas Affair 104

IX. Écrasez l'Infâme 111

X. The End 125

Bibliography 136

Index 138

I

CRADLE TO BASTILLE

The child that was to be Voltaire came into the world at Paris on November 21st, 1694. It was not expected to live, and was baptized at home. The man who was to deny all miracles was a perpetual miracle in his own person. Always oscillating between death and life, Voltaire found the contrast so stimulating, that he defied public opinion, in this as in all else, by surviving, with undiminished zest in life, to the age of eighty-four. In this long term he enjoyed every experience save boredom. Never well, and often at the point of death, he none the less contrived to work with a steady industry that few, even of the dullest men, have equalled. One is curious about the physical endowment of this unusual personality, but little, save the visible externals, can be gathered from the records. The portraits and statues have made us all familiar with the meagre little body, graceful perhaps in youth, emaciated in middle life, a skeleton in the last thirty years. Nature wasted nothing in superfluous muscle. He aged prematurely, and half-way through the fifties he speaks of himself as an old man. Yet to the end this mummy preserved its incredible mental activity. Out of its toothless jaws came verses, epigrams and masterpieces of irresponsible fun that sparkle with the gaiety of youth. This perpetual invalid was never idle, and the only difference in his output seems to have been, that when he was really seriously ill, he wrote verse instead of prose.

What was the secret of this perpetual youth? Perhaps it lay in his physical instability. His temperament rushed at the smallest provocation through all the extremes of emotion. He was by turns gentle and irascible: some offences he would pardon with a negligent charity, while others roused him to uncontrollable malignity: usually talkative and gay, he had his moods of sulky silence: usually graceful and courtly in his manners, he could behave with brutal rudeness: sensitive to suffering as few men have ever been, he none the less performed one or two cruel actions: prodigally generous on many occasions with his money, he could be grasping like any French peasant: cautious and prudent in the face of physical danger, he could be stirred to combative fury: bending to any storm, ready at any moment to retract or apologize, he always rebounded, and lived to fight with renewed militancy the next day. Yet this unstable, excitable, quarrelsome man was a constant and devoted lover, and kept to the end the friends of his youth. His opinions grew in firmness, but never changed their direction, while he worked with the accuracy and discipline of an intellectual puritan. A modern physician, putting together the few ill-observed facts that can be gleaned, would probably class him as an extreme allergic. But no medical diagnosis will exhaust this miracle. Intellect, working above this temperamental volcano, shaped the firm outlines of his mental life.

The little boy, François-Marie Arouet, vivacious, wilful and precocious, grew up in a typical home of the middle class, as the fortunes of the family were rising. Little is known of it, for it reached distinction only in this one individual. The Arouets came from Poitou; several of them were tanners, and one a draper who settled and throve in Paris. Voltaire's father was a lawyer, who had several great families as his clients, those of Sully and Richelieu among them. Both opened their doors to his brilliant son in his early years, and the Duke of Richelieu became his lifelong friend. The family was sociable and saw what was called 'good company'. The father had met the poet Corneille and found him very dull. The mother, who came of a legal family of much the same rank, was a friend in her youth of the gay and brilliant Ninon de Lenclos, who left the boy a small legacy with which to buy books. An intimate of the house was the Abbé de Châteauneuf, a notable wit and freethinker of this period, who wrote polished verses and took an interest in the education of his godson, little Francis. It was none the less a serious home, for Voltaire's father was a Jansenist, albeit moderate in his opinions, while his elder brother, Armand, professed the faith of the family with fanaticism. The father may have been a man of some ability, not without culture, but his values, as we shall see, were those of his creed.

Jansenism, as its orthodox foes insisted, had much in common with Calvinism. It was an authentic Catholic belief: it based itself on St. Augustine and would not quit the City of God, the universal Church. None the less it was a subjective religion, which stressed 'grace' above 'works'. It emphasized the necessity of a sudden act of conversion. Grace, at the predestined moment, descends like a whirlwind, but only on the few elect. A penitential discipline, however, must follow the call to grace, under the direction of an expert confessor, so severe and absorbing that all else becomes vanity—the arts, literature, family ties, even civic duty. This doctrine of other-worldliness led straight to the monastery, and indeed, as the pious biographer of M. de Saint-Cyran, the chief organizer and evangelist of the sect in France, said of his hero, he strove 'happily to depeople earth and give new citizens to Heaven'. Like Protestant Nonconformists, the Jansenists were much given to the study of the scriptures, and like them also they tended to become a loosely organized party of opposition, at feud with Church and State, and driven to insist, as persecution weighed upon them, upon their liberties. They were Gallican nationalists, always at war with Rome. Their moral standards were exacting, and they enforced them by rigid rules of frequent communion, and severe penance, whereas their arch-enemies, the Jesuits, were content to get a man on easy terms to the confessional, satisfied that the magic of absolution would save his soul. Doubtless there were Tartuffes among these puritans, but they will live in literature as much in the exalted, self-tormenting sincerity of Pascal's *Pensées* (Thoughts) as in Molière's caricature. They were of the most characteristic manifestation of French middle-class life in Voltaire's day, and the background out of which he emerged. All over Europe, the middle class, as it rose to wealth and aspired to power, created for itself this grave religious atmosphere, in which conduct was schooled for the serious business of life, and all the passions and vanities repressed. Whatever doctrinal differences divided Jansenists from Calvinists, their temper and outlook were curiously alike. They even affected the same outward uniform of sad-coloured clothes. Savage persecution had stopped the growth of the Huguenot Church in France some years before Voltaire was born, but nothing could check the tendency of the middle class, at this stage of its ascent, towards some form of Puritanism. From the first, Jansenists worked miracles and encouraged faith-healing: in their later phases they degenerated into an ecstatic revivalism. Voltaire's was the temperament that inherits by reacting. He won freedom and made his own career only by revolting against his Jansenist father, and nothing in his writings is quite so manifestly felt as his continuous polemic against other-worldliness. But something, none the less, Voltaire may have gained directly from this Nonconformist party. His boyhood fell in the dark years of Louis XIV's reign. As one defeat after another struck that monarch's armies, he seems to have believed that he could propitiate Heaven and save himself another Blenheim only by exterminating the enemies of the Church. Protestants he massacred with ferocity, and these Catholic heretics were not spared a milder form of persecution. Voltaire was a boy of fifteen when their monastic college of Port Royal was demolished, and a plough driven through the cemetery where lay their sainted dead. The boy had no liking for saints, but he hated persecution with a passion that had its roots in his earliest memories.

The boy's mother died when he was seven years of age. His father was a harsh man, rough in his manners, and given to scolding. His elder brother was antipathetic, and the affections of this sensitive child turned to his elder sister Margaret, afterwards Madame Mignot. The father had now bought a lucrative place in the Exchequer, and the family inhabited an official residence in the centre of the city. At the age of ten the boy was sent to the Jesuit college, Louis le Grand. Why his Jansenist father chose this school one does not know, unless for the simple reason that the Jesuits were at this time incomparably the best teachers in Europe. This was their most distinguished school, and in some sense the social centre of their party. They were now at the height of their power, and in effect governed France through Le Tellier, Louis' confessor. The sons of the great crowded this fashionable school, at which boys made connections in the ruling faction that were valuable in after life. Noblemen's sons had their own rooms, with valets and tutors to attend them. The commoners lived five to a room, with a prefect, a priest, to watch over them. The discipline was severe: flogging was not infrequent and occasionally there was riotous resistance. The fathers gave a good classical education, but they were far in advance of their age in the attention they paid to French literature and history. In after-life Voltaire, even while he was at open war with the Order, wrote with gratitude and affection about his teachers. They led, he said, 'austere and laborious lives', and gave him a taste for 'letters and virtue'. He won every possible prize, played no games and consorted rather with the masters than the boys. He rhymed with great ease, and even while he was a schoolboy some of his verses went the round of the drawing-rooms of Paris. His chief interest, however, lay, even at this time, in history and contemporary politics. He made at school some valuable friendships with boys who afterwards held high office and gave him some little protection in his numerous quarrels with authority.

The boy left college at 16, determined to follow a literary career. His father, declaring that literature is useless and leads only to starvation, sent him to a law school. He refused to take the smallest interest in law, neglected his classes, and rejected his father's offer to set him up for life by buying him a post as one of the King's Counsel. Because he was leading what his Jansenist family considered a dissipated life, his father first sent him out of Paris to vegetate at Caen, and then (1713) procured for him a very junior diplomatic post in the suite of the Marquis de Châteauneuf, the Abbé's brother, who had been appointed French Minister at the Hague. 'Dissipation' is a relative term. Doubtless the youth was vain, wore fashionable clothes, kept late hours, enjoyed lively company and wrote naughty verses, but he was much too intelligent for the coarser forms of pleasure, and much too delicate for heavy drinking. Even at this time he was a systematic worker, and was already writing, re-writing and for ever polishing his first tragedy in verse. His stay at the Hague was short, and is chiefly notable for an innocent adventure that ended his diplomatic career. At 19 he fell in love, for the first time, with a young woman, Olympe Dunoyer, somewhat older and more experienced than himself, whom he was bent on marrying. She was unfortunately the daughter of a clever, notorious French

Protestant refugee, who published a venomous sheet called *Quintessence*, which collected every fragment of news and scandal calculated to injure the cause of Catholic France. 'Pimpette', indeed, had previously been engaged to Colonel Jean Cavalier, the gallant soldier who first led the revolted Protestants of the Cevennes, and then carried a troop of them into Queen Anne's service in the Flanders wars. A less suitable mate for a young French diplomatist could hardly have been found, while Madame Dunoyer on her side looked higher. The Minister, when this indiscretion was brought to his notice, placed the young man under arrest and packed him off to Paris at the first opportunity. There was, however, an interval of a few days in which the pair contrived to enjoy the excitement of romance. They smuggled letters to each other, and Pimpette, who wrote with unmistakable passion and a touch of maternal tenderness, had the enterprise to disguise herself as a boy and visit her imprisoned lover. Voltaire, if he was the less impassioned, was the more constant of the two. He went on conspiring, long after his enforced return to Paris, to arrange an elopement. The lady, however, consoled herself with a titled husband.

This escapade infuriated the father, who threatened to send his son to America, but eventually placed him in the office of a notary. Here Voltaire neglected his duties and went on writing poetry, but his quick wits enabled him, without much effort, to pick up a fair amount of legal knowledge and to grasp the technique of business. Few poets have possessed, as he did, the secret of making money with equal prudence and facility. In this office, was another young man of like tastes, Thiériot, with whom he formed a friendship that lasted through life. This phase in the poet's career was brief. A veteran statesman, M. de Caumartin, now Marquis de Saint-Ange, took pity on him, and persuaded his father to allow him to leave the office and keep him company at his château near Fontainebleau. Caumartin's boast was that he knew everything, open or hidden, that had happened in the Court and administration of Louis XIV, and while he gossiped, Voltaire took copious notes. It was his habit throughout life to work at several books at once, and already, though his immediate concern was poetry, he was gathering material for his history of the past century. About this time his godfather, the

Abbé Châteauneuf, introduced him to the society of the Temple.
This was a dining club, over which the Abbé Chaulieu presided.
It was a gathering of wits, who had hammered out among themselves a code of literary taste, which their prestige imposed on Paris.
There were among them several princes of the blood, but most of
them were abbés and all were dissolute. The brilliant youth had
now and always the art of mixing with his elders and social superiors
without the handicap of modesty. He caught the atmosphere of this
circle, and his early poems reflect it. These graceful verses of social
life are among the best in their kind that this century produced.
They flow like spontaneous talk, though in fact every line was
polished with elaborate care. Letters to friends, portrait sketches,
moralizings, compliments to fair ladies, flattery for princes, thanks
to actresses who played his tragedies—they ran incessantly from his
pen, and those that he wrote in old age are as graceful as the flowers
of his youth. They reflect the society in which he lived, complacent,
limited, content to enjoy its luxuries and its elegance, proud of its
theatre and Poussin's pictures, its silks and its sparkling wines, light
in its loves, troubled by no mysteries, sure of itself because it knew
the steps of the formal dance that was its life. It was a period of ex-
pansion and unrestrained enjoyment. Louis XIV, who had turned to
a gloomy and superstitious piety in his old age, was dead (1715).
The Regent, Philip of Orleans, was the model of self-indulgence,
and he brought back from exile and prison the more dissolute priests
and the more turbulent nobles whom the old king had banished.
Soon Law was printing the paper money that was to make everyone
rich. Oddly enough, the wits of the Temple, whose empty chairs
filled up again as the prisons opened their doors, turned on the
Regent and 'his Messalina of a daughter', and assailed his morals
with a flood of epigrams and lampoons, that ran through all the
drawing-rooms of Paris, and kept the secret-police busy tracking
down the anonymous authors. The writing of witty satires in verse
was in this century the national sport of the French, a form of
sadism more refined than the bull-baiting of Spain, but calculated to
satisfy the same deep-seated instincts. The bull marked down for
every ambitious picador was at this moment the Regent, and Voltaire
must needs throw his darts with the rest. By way of warning, he was

banished on suspicion from Paris. He went as a guest to the magnificent ducal castle of Sully, where he wrote and enjoyed himself by turns, and found a pretty mistress. It was not a harsh punishment, judged by the ways of that century, but Voltaire returned to the capital bent on revenge. The secret-service reports show that he went about boasting the authorship of several of the current libels on the Regent. He was in fact innocent of the one which the authorities chiefly resented (a satire, beginning '*J'ai vu*'), but he did write some peculiarly libellous Latin verses beginning *Puero regnante* which were found when his rooms were searched (May 1717). He raged against the Regent, as the police carried him off to the Bastille, and there he lay, as the custom of that place was, untried, at the Crown's pleasure for eleven months. He was not ill treated. He had his own room and his books, and he dined at the governor's table, where the company was usually good, for it was not the stupider half of French society that found itself in opposition. The records show that he sent out for what he chiefly needed— a night-cap, a bottle of scent and two volumes of Homer. He was neither idle nor depressed, and in his cell he wrote the greater part of the *Henriade*, which one may describe as the epic of royalist liberalism. An exile of a further eleven months out of Paris completed his punishment. To us it seems a heavy infliction to impose on a very young man for some bitter yet just verses which in fact he did not write, but it was mild treatment by the standards of this age. A poet who wrote a deserved satire on Louis XV for his meanness towards the Young Pretender was kept for six years in an iron cage on Mont Saint Michel.

While the poet was still nominally in exile, his first tragedy, *Œdipe*, was acted at the Comédie Française. It was already well known by private readings to the fashionable world, and everyone but the actors thought well of it. It achieved an immense success, and had a 'run', unparalleled in those days, of forty-five nights. The opposition hailed it with particular delight and cheered to the echo some rather trite anti-clerical sentiments put into Jocasta's mouth. The theme of incest also was topical, since this was the charge that the picadors threw at the Regent. The young man's audacity took Paris by storm. He had challenged not only Sophocles but Corneille, who had written a rather inferior play on this subject, and by general consent he had won in the contest. As Voltaire went on adding one polished tragedy to another, fame placed him third among the masters of the French classical stage.

His plays are neglected today save in the repertory of old-fashioned schools, but they were in his own lifetime the foundation of his influence and prestige. Of nothing were the French of this age so proud as of their theatre. England might shine in science and Italy in the arts, but France, after the long night of Gothic darkness, had revived and surpassed the glories of the Attic stage. It was a very young civilization, and an uneasy sense of its own inferiority had weighed upon it, until it convinced itself that Corneille and Racine had beaten the Greeks on their own ground. The theatre had, under an absolute monarchy, a unique position that it lost with the advent of democracy. Within these walls took place the nearest available substitute for a public meeting. A daring couplet of Voltaire's, as later an epigram by Beaumarchais, became a political event. A republican sentiment declaimed by an actor in a toga moved all Paris more profoundly than did any oration by Danton in later days. A clever writer knew just how much he might risk, for the police wrote elaborate reports on every first night—and the quick ears of the capital missed no chance of a demonstration. One asks oneself, when one views against the despotism of this century the incredible audacities of Voltaire, how this man survived? The answer is that he was recognized not in France only, but in Europe, as the greatest dramatist of his day. He brought glory to the language and civilization of a proud nation that had in this century few victories of which to boast. His other works, with few exceptions, were printed abroad to be smuggled into France, and some were burned by the public executioner. His plays alone were freely published, and some were even acted at Court. They gave him what, under an even more brutal despotism, his novels won for Tolstoy, the right when all others were silenced, to speak his mind.

The first difficulty in forming an estimate of Voltaire's plays is that we must read what he intended us to hear and see. The rhymed alexandrines must not mislead us: these are stage plays. Voltaire had a passion for amateur acting: it was, with chess, his only relaxation, and by all accounts he did it well, though with an excess of vivacity. Wherever in his wandering life he settled for any length of time, a room in his house was fitted as a theatre. He thought in terms of movement on the stage, and his first concern was to devise, within the rules of the unities, a play that would act well. His plots are admirably constructed, his exits and entrances carefully arranged, and as one reads, disappointed by the aridity and the forensic monotony of the dialogue, one pulls oneself up with a jerk to realize that the piece, if one can succeed in visualizing it, is a most effective melodrama. The aridity was deliberate. There are rhetorical passages that great actors rejoiced to declaim, but even these are swift, terse and economical. Never will he digress into the relief of pure poetry. Sometimes he followed a Greek model, and one act of his *Œdipe*, though he improves on Athens by introducing an elegant, triangular sex complication, is almost a free translation from Sophocles. But like his predecessors, he discarded the chorus, and never are we lifted, as the Greeks lift us, above the terror and tension of the stage, by the verbal magic of great lyrics, into the free world of beauty. Voltaire could admire with many reserves the poetical digressions in Shakespeare's plays, but for himself he would never delay by one superfluous line the swift development of the action. The result is that no memorable passages haunt the memory, when we have read a play, though many a line stands out by the directness and aptness of its statement. He enslaved himself, as Lessing, in this case a malicious critic, pointed out, even more pedantically than Corneille to the unities. He dreaded any touch of homeliness (as he explains in the preface to *Mérope*), any lapse into familiarity, as unworthy of the dignity of tragedy. He never unbends, and it is typical of his taste that he damned the gravediggers' scene in *Hamlet* as barbarism. Tragedy must never drop the heroic mask. To a modern ear his dialogues are stilted, and even in a highly emotional passage his heroes and heroines use abstract terms for choice. This was not his natural manner of writing, for in his tales the whole effect is often reached by the startling use of the simplest concrete words. Since all the persons of his tragedies must talk this uniform heroic dialect, there is no subtlety, hardly indeed any individuality in the drawing of character.

Voltaire's highest praise for a dramatist is, as he says of Dryden, that he could write 'a reasonable tragedy'. The madness, the exaltation of an experience that transforms or shatters one's universe were not for him. The difficulty of the modern reader is to convince himself that these themes drawn from an alien mythology (*Œdipe* and *Mérope*) or from the remote Middle Ages (*Zaïre*, *Tancred* and *Mahomed*) have any relation to an experience that was ever real. There is no attempt to reproduce the ways of thought of a bygone age, yet the motives and actions of these persons would be incredible in our own. That applies to the French classical drama generally, but more consciously than its other masters, Voltaire was competing—treating a subject, as he supposes, more nobly, or more ingeniously than his predecessors, from Sophocles to Crébillon, had treated it. These plays are exercises in the classical manner: they were not written under the compulsion of any direct experience or any strong feeling. To this general criticism there is one exception. He must have been reading Las Casas when he wrote *Alzire*, and this play about Spaniards and Incas has life in it, because it is inspired by the deepest of Voltaire's feelings, his hatred of cruelty. Through the neat versification and the stilted language and in spite of the edifying and improbable ending, the flame of this passion reaches us, and at moments scorches us. None the less, one respects these monuments of industry, for most of them were written and reshaped several times over. One admires the skilful construction and the smooth versification, and rebukes oneself for one's coldness, as one recollects that no less a judge than Goethe found *Tancred* worthy the honour of translation.

The production of *Œdipe* in 1717 marks an epoch in Voltaire's life. He was now, at 22, the rising literary genius of his day. He chose the moment to adopt the name by which posterity knows him. He had no ties that he valued with the Arouet family and he did what Molière before him had done, and Balzac and Anatole France after him were to do. It is not quite certain whence he drew his new name. Probably it was an anagram of Arouet junior (Arouet l.j.), but some say without evidence that he took it from a farm belonging to his family, while others will have it that it was an abbreviation of a nickname, 'le volontaire' (Master Wilful) that he bore at school. The Regent, on the whole a good-natured sinner, gave him a medal and a pension for *Œdipe*. Voltaire, in thanking him, begged that His Highness, while kindly providing in future for his keep, 'would not again charge himself with his lodging'. His father died in 1722 and left him an income sufficient for a young bachelor. He writes more tragedies, spends his summers at the castles of great nobles (the exiled Bolingbroke among them), travels on a semi-official diplomatic mission to the Low Countries in the company of a brilliant adventuress, Madame de Rupelmonde, writes in her honour one of his most famous and most challenging poems, the *Letter to Urania*, a manifesto of sceptical hedonism, is feasted by princes and generals at the French headquarters in Cambrai, and opens with the lyric poet J. B. Rousseau (not the more famous Jaques) the first of his innumerable literary feuds. It raged for some years, with some wit and more brutality, and divided all Paris into two camps. Rousseau, a libertine and a sceptic in early life, had turned to piety in his old age. He took the liberty of scolding Voltaire for writing sceptical verses, whereupon the latter in his irritation doubted whether Rousseau's *Ode to Posterity* 'would ever reach its destination'. These quarrels of Voltaire's hardly deserve our attention today. They are significant only because they are the froth of a turmoil that meant something vital for history. Voltaire might start a quarrel by a chance thrust at a pompous old man with his irrepressible verbal rapier, but the old man and his journalistic backers had now their chance to hold up the poet to execration and punishment as a sceptic and a radical. The armament of the two parties was unequal. Voltaire had nothing but his wit, while the orthodox had their rearguard in the Bastille and the censor's office.

The shadow of these two places was over him again. He had now finished his *Henriade* (entitled in this first version, *The League*) and had been refused a licence for its publication. Nothing daunted, he had it printed clandestinely, for the commercial purveyors of intellectual intoxicants were in these days as rash, as adventurous, as grasping and as rascally as any modern 'boot-legger'. The smuggled edition had an enormous success. Everyone wanted it because it was forbidden. Besides, it flattered the national pride of this self-conscious, adolescent civilization, that a French poet had at last written an epic, and taken as his hero the gallant Henri IV, the best beloved, the most Gallic of all the kings of France. It is a poem in the Latin tradition. Here is proportion, good form, a solid architecture, sustained competence, but no rash brilliance, no moments either of relaxation or exaltation. The speeches are rather better than the narrative and display what the poet himself would have called a male eloquence. The tendency of this emphatically propagandist poem is interesting, though it is far from disclosing the whole of Voltaire's mind. His purpose is to raise a monument to the first national patriot, the first tolerant king who aspired to be the father of all his people. He reveals his liberalism (much accentuated in the later version) and his international sympathies by his flattering portrait of Queen Elizabeth and his eulogy of English institutions. It was bold to make a hero of the Huguenot Coligny, and bolder still to insert an unsparing narrative of the massacre of Saint Bartholomew, for that exploit had been consecrated by the striking of a Papal medal and the approval of the theologians of the Sorbonne. Though the smuggled poem ended with a glowing vision of the grandeurs of Louis XIV's reign, the orthodox were not placated, and if Voltaire now ranked as the first living poet of France, he had climbed to a more dangerous eminence, for he was felt to be the pioneer of the subversive opposition.

At the height of his success, in the last days of 1725, there happened to him a misfortune that altered the whole tenor of his life. While talking one evening at the Opera with his usual spirit and confidence in the company of the greatest actress of this period, Mlle. Lecouvreur, whom he tenderly admired, an aristocrat came up and drawled at him a stupid insult: 'M. de Voltaire, M. Arouet, what's your name?' The poet took no notice, but next evening the same gentleman repeated the same pleasantry. He was the Chevalier de Rohan, a soldier who never fought a battle, a man who had lived through forty years without other distinction than the right to bear one of the greatest names in the history of France. This time Voltaire had his answer, and it was not without dignity: 'The name I bear is not a great one, but I at least know how to bring it honour.'

The Chevalier raised his cane, but did not actually strike. Voltaire put his hand on his sword hilt. The lady tactfully fainted, and so ended the incident for the moment.

Two or three days later a message reached Voltaire inviting him to dine at the Sully mansion. In this there was nothing surprising, but in fact the Duke had sent no invitation. Half-way through dinner, a messenger asked for Voltaire at the street door. A coach stood there in which was the Chevalier de Rohan, who directed six of his men while they mercilessly cudgelled his victim. Escaping at last into the house, Voltaire begged the Duke to accompany him to the commissioner of police. In spite of an intimacy of ten years, the Duke refused this service: the family of Rohan was too powerful to offend. Voltaire had now to realize that in the great world of his day a plebeian who suffered a beating was an object not of sympathy but of derision. 'We should be most unfortunate,' said a noble Bishop, when he heard of this outrage, 'if poets had no shoulders.' Such affairs were not uncommon: Dryden had been beaten by Lord Rochester's negro lackey. This century described itself as the age of politeness and in its less ruffled moments it did attain in intercourse between equals an exquisite grace. Politeness was certainly its ideal, which means that it consciously strove to reach by effort a grace that was far from spontaneous. The substratum, the natural, uncensored course of its behaviour was still an instinctive brutality. Louis XV was now on his throne, no longer a minor, and his queen had recently bestowed a pension on Voltaire. He applied to the Ministry for redress, only to meet with a blank refusal. Voltaire was not physically a brave man, but there was now no way of escaping public contempt save by a duel. The police reports describe his desperate excitement: he took lessons in fencing, found a second, delivered his challenge, and expected a meeting next day. The owners of great names do not cross swords with middle-class poets. The Rohan family stepped in and had Voltaire arrested. Once more (April 17th, 1726) he found himself in the Bastille. His stay was brief. This time he was determined to place himself out of reach of this institution. By his own request he was escorted to Calais, and there he took the packet for England. This experience cut deep. He did not cease to make his way among the great. With all his assurance, he did not yet know his own powers, and for many years he stooped to make use of kings and queens, English and Polish, Prussian and even French. But his writings show that the Rohan cudgel had left its mark. It consecrated him thinker to the middle-class revolution.

II

EXILE IN ENGLAND

Straight from the Bastille, Voltaire came with quick eyes and a receptive mind into a world of happy contrasts. His first impressions were favourable. He landed on a brilliant sunny day of spring to find, for it was Whit-Monday and the King's birthday, Greenwich in festival. The King, to the accompaniment of water-music, was visiting the Thames, and his barge rowed in procession between six miles of ships in full sail. The exile, struck by the gaiety of the common people at the fair and the good looks of the women, drew from this smiling scene an impression of universal liberty and abundance. He began from his first day to realize the importance of commerce and a merchant marine in the wealth of nations.

The stranger was well received. Bolingbroke, who had been his host while an exile in France, was now at home again, and introduced him to his literary circle, Swift, Pope and Gay. These happy impressions faded, however, for a time. The climate tried him, and the east wind withered him. Haunted by the memory of his humiliation, he crept secretly back to France for several weeks in a vain effort to force de Rohan to a duel. Soon after his return, his beloved sister died, and his letters reflect the misery of his affectionate nature. He could find no consolation: 'It is only magicians who pretend to calm storms with words.' He sought oblivion in work, and began his wide reading of the whole range of English literature, not poetry alone, but history, science, even sermons. He was miserably poor, for his banker, one d'Acosta, had gone bankrupt, and he had lost, by one account, as much as 20,000 francs on a letter of change. He found life in England expensive: servants in the houses of the great had to be handsomely tipped, and there were also doctors' bills. But his fame had gone before him, and he met with much kindness. George I, hearing of his loss, sent him a hundred guineas. The Bolingbrokes offered to help him, but he refused their aid 'because they are lords', and preferred the hospitality of a simple commoner, one Everard Falkener, whom he had met, though only once in Paris. Voltaire at this time spoke of himself as a 'republican'. This Falkener, who had a country house at Wandsworth, was a wealthy retired merchant, an unusual character, public-spirited, at home among books, and a model of kindliness and generosity. In later life he was knighted and entered the public service, first as Ambassador at the Sublime Porte, and then as Postmaster-General, a promotion that made a deep impression on Voltaire, as a proof of the political consequence of his class. It is a just possible guess that Falkener sat for his portrait as the blunt, eccentric, benevolent merchant in Voltaire's curious comedy of London life, *L'Ecossaise*. Voltaire, while he made his way in the world of letters and fashion and was even presented at Court, frequented even more gladly the homes of the middle class. One supposes that he must have met several Quakers: one of them, a patriarch named Andrew Pitt, he interrogated systematically about their beliefs. He met and greatly admired Newton's versatile disciple and translator, Samuel Clarke, Rector of St. James's, scholar, theologian and physicist. He had at this time hardly grasped the attitude of the empirical English mind towards metaphysics. Remarking one day to an acquaintance that Dr. Clarke was an even greater metaphysician than Newton, he was startled when the Englishman replied: 'That is much as if you were to say that the one plays more skilfully with toy balloons than the other.' In the literary world he seems to have met almost everyone worth meeting. Of all save one he wrote afterwards with friendly respect. It was inevitable that he and Samuel Johnson should disapprove of one another, but the anecdotes that Johnson reports in the *Lives of the Poets* are certainly inaccurate and probably malicious. The story that he horrified Pope and Swift by his impiety and indelicacy, and drove Pope's old mother from the dinner-table, contains one gross anachronism and several improbabilities. Voltaire went on writing affectionately in after years to the whole circle: he admired and liked 'Sir Homère' and 'Sir Ovide', as he playfully called Pope and Gay. Some momentary coldness and suspicion there doubtless was, for Voltaire, like a wise explorer, moved impartially between Tory and Whig circles, and was welcomed in both the rival Courts of George I and the Prince of Wales. Congreve he admired as a dramatist, but felt less respect for the fine gentleman. The Whig poets, at least, notably Thomson and Young, found him entertaining, piquant, and agreeably shocking, for that is the impression conveyed by Young's impromptu epigram. After Voltaire had argued hotly that Milton's allegory of Death and Sin is in bad taste, the author of *Night Thoughts*, who was evidently genuinely attached to him, scribbled this couplet:

> You are so witty, profligate and thin,
> At once we think you Milton, Death and Sin.

He paid some lengthy visits to country houses, and he had valuable talks over recent history with the old Duchess of Marlborough at Blenheim. When he asked her to lend him her manuscript memoirs, she put him off with the deliciously frank answer: 'Wait a bit: I'm reshaping the character of Queen Anne, since I've begun to like her again.'

Voltaire's stay was evidently as pleasant as it was profitable. He even meditated settling in England. 'In this country,' he wrote to his friend Thiériot, 'it is possible to use one's mind freely and nobly without fear and cringing. If I followed my own inclinations, I should stay here, if only to learn how to think.' He mastered the language thoroughly. He tells us that he came to think in English. He could make an impromptu speech and, indeed, on one occasion used this gift to turn an untoward adventure into a triumph. London swarmed at this time with Huguenot refugees, who made Frenchmen excessively unpopular with the masses by their readiness to work at less than the prevailing rates of wages. Some workers, detecting Voltaire's nationality as he walked the streets, began throwing mud at him. He made them a flattering and amusing speech. 'Is it not misfortune enough for me,' he began, 'that I was not born among you?' and went on until they chaired him and carried him in triumph to his lodgings. Life, even in England, had its risks and shadows. On one occasion a Thames waterman insulted him, telling him that all Frenchmen were slaves. Next day he saw the fellow in the grip of the press-gang.

Voltaire began to sketch his play *Brutus* in English prose, and published two essays on epic poetry and the French civil wars which show a perfect mastery of English style. A set of verses that he wrote to Lady Hervey, though trite enough, are as rhythmic and idiomatic as one could wish.

Voltaire, meanwhile, did not neglect his own studies. He wrote in England the most spirited and popular of his historical works, *The History of Charles XII*, a task on which he spent much labour. He reshaped and indeed rewrote his epic, the *Henriade*, profiting as he always did by every criticism that reached him, whether from friend or foe. The book that had to be clandestinely printed in France was published in England with a dedication that the Queen accepted, couched in respectful but decidedly Whiggish language. Among the subscribers were all the more cultured of the nobility, and Voltaire reaped a modest fortune from its sale. Part of the edition was smuggled into France as packing paper.

Voltaire spent nearly three years in England, but in truth, for the rest of his days, he was always there. He said in after years that though he had named his study of the past epoch 'the century of Louis XIV', he might have called it more appropriately 'the English Century'. This land of tolerance, inquiry and freedom had become his spiritual home, and he never tired to the end of his long life of dwelling on the virtues of the English character and the sagacity of English institutions, in a way that Frenchmen must have found not a little irritating. Montesquieu, who came to England a few months after Voltaire's departure and spent eighteen months there, did the same thing in a somewhat more sober way. Rousseau, on the other hand, an introvert who spoke no English, was miserable and gained nothing from his stay. French Liberalism, though it developed on its own daringly original lines, was in its origin inspired by England.

Voltaire was stimulated by this free, positive society, and derived from it a new orientation to life. His wit remained; he still 'considered solemnity a disease'; but the frivolity of his youth disappeared. Of this inner change he was himself perfectly conscious. 'Forget,' he wrote to Thiériot, speaking of his early writings, 'Forget all these deliriums of my youth. For my part I have drunk of the River Lethe. I remember nothing but my friends.' He had escaped from the trivialities of the Temple dinner-table into the atmosphere of the Royal Society. His whole scale of values changed. Life, from his stay in England onward, now meant for him primarily three things. First came the intoxicating adventure of scientific discovery, which included not merely the firm demonstration of new truths in physics, optics or chemistry, but the dazzling vision of a rational, systematic universe. This was for him an English idea: it came to him from Newton. Second only to this new perception of rational system in the universe came an interest in material progress, and Voltaire begins to dwell on the importance of commerce and manufacture, and of the middle class as the pioneer in a general effort of improvement, in phrases that at times recall Defoe. Lastly, though experience had taught him between his two stays in the Bastille all that a young man need know about the humiliations and perils of life under a despotism, it was on English soil that he dug down to some, at least, of the foundations of freedom. His was a positive mind that took no interest in 'chimæras'. But freedom he had seen and experienced; this, then, was an attainable goal.

His exile ended in March 1729, but he had still to spend a period of quarantine outside Paris, and he settled at St. Germains. His head full of England, he sat down to complete his record of his impressions. These *Philosophical Letters* cover with a pompous title a gay and spirited little book, which some have even called superficial. Voltaire had his good reasons for adopting this tone, and they explain much else in his writing, and, indeed, in the whole literary output of the French Liberals. If one wished to survive in the shadow of the Bastille, one must not deliver a frontal attack with knitted brows and taut muscles. Negligently, lightly, with an air of saying nothing of importance, one may contrive to hint at half one's thought between two peals of laughter. Voltaire, before he risked the publication of these explosive letters, had tested their effect on the authorities by reading them to the prime minister, Cardinal Fleury, a limited but easy-going personage, who condescended to be amused. A Frenchman, even if he be a Cardinal, must laugh even at a blasphemy if it be witty enough. It does not follow, however, that he will continue to laugh, a fact which Voltaire forgot. There was no blasphemies in the *Letters*, but there were thrusts of a fearless wit at every French institution—the Church, the clergy, the nobility, the system of taxation, even the immortal Academy. Worse than this, the total effect was to present a picture of a society enviably free, striding to great influence and wealth, and incomparably more advanced than France in the essentials of civilization. The little book is slight, if one compares it with such contemporary studies of English and American life as M. André Siegfried has written. It was not Voltaire's purpose to convey exact information. His readers would draw from this sketch no very precise idea of what the English constitution was, or how in detail parliamentary institutions worked. His aim was rather to present a selection of sketches that it would be salutary for Frenchmen to contemplate. Much more might have been said with advantage. It is remarkable that the book contains nothing about the English Deists, an omission made good in later works. Much, Voltaire tells us, was cut from his first draft about Locke, the Quakers and the Presbyterians. His 'heart bled' as he did it, 'but after all I want to live in France'.

The book is not all propaganda. Much of it is designed to entertain. Though Voltaire felt a sympathy for the Quakers in remarkable contrast to his coldness towards all other Protestant sects save the Unitarians, he certainly was not trying to kindle the inner light in Catholic breasts. But in his account of the multiplicity of sects in England he did mean to draw attention to the happy consequences of toleration. 'An Englishman,' he tells us, 'being a free man, goes to heaven by the road of his choice. . . . Had there been only one religion in England, its despotism would have been formidable: had there been only two, they would have cut each other's throats: but there are thirty, and they live happy and at peace.' He permits himself a double-edged jest at the clergy: they have retained many Catholic ceremonies, above all that of collecting tithes with the most scrupulous punctuality. They like to be masters in their villages, but they have had to submit to the authority of Parliament. They are, on the whole, monogamous, and if they ever get drunk, they do it seriously and without scandal. 'When they learn that in France young fellows, notorious for their debauchery, raised to their bishoprics by women's intrigues, make love in public, amuse themselves by composing tender lyrics, spread daily and at length a luxurious dinner, and go from it to pray for the guidance of the Holy Ghost, while they boldly claim to be the successors of the apostles, Englishmen thank God that they are Protestants. But then, as Master Rabelais said, they are miserable heretics, fit only to be burned, the devil take them, and that is why I leave them to their own affairs.'

Voltaire's tone becomes graver when he writes about political liberty in England. He makes a half apology for the execution of Charles I, and contrasts our fruitful civil strife with the prolonged internal wars of the French, which only tightened their chains. 'The English nation is the only one on this earth that has contrived to regulate the power of kings by resisting them. By one effort after another it finally established this wise system of government which leaves the prince all-powerful to do good, but ties his hands, if he be minded to do ill. Without vassals, the nobles are great without insolence, and the people share in the government without disorder.'

There follows a bold historical summary of the steps that led to the breaking of the feudal system in England. In his account of Parliament, he dwells somewhat literally on the Commons' power over the King's purse, hardly perceiving its significance as a means of controlling policy. For him it means little more than a protection against arbitrary taxation. In this book, as in his graver historical works, it is the defensive motives of the rising middle class that he stresses, whether he is dealing with the Protestant Reformation, the Gallican movement, or the struggles for political power. It was safe-guarding its property against Popes and Kings; the rest was incidental. This frank realism of his is invaluable to the student of history. Cradled in a Jansenist family, born again in the England of the glorious Whig revolution, himself the forerunner of the French Revolution, he knew by instinct and intercourse the mind of the middle class to which he gave the most brilliant literary expression. Peter's pence, ship money, the annates of the French bishoprics, the salt gabelle—these economic grievances are the starting-points in the long international struggle of the middle class, and one might complete the list with the Boston tea-party. Here is the peroration

of Voltaire's account of English liberty: every phrase conveys an in-
direct criticism of French conditions. 'A man, because he is noble,
or because he is a priest, is not on that account exempt from paying
certain taxes: all the taxes are fixed by the House of Commons,
which though it is only the second in rank, is the first in influence.

'The lords and the bishops may reject a money bill of the commons, but they cannot amend it. Everyone pays: each gives, not
according to his rank (for that would be absurd) but according to his
income: there is no personal tax ("taille"), no arbitrary poll-tax,
but a real tax on landed properties: these were valued under the
famous King William III at a figure below their market price.

'The tax remains invariable, though the income from the land
may have increased: accordingly no one is harried, and no one
complains. The peasant's feet are not bruised by sabots; he eats
white bread; he is well-clad; he does not hesitate to increase the
number of his cattle, or to cover his roof with tiles, from fear lest his
taxes be raised the next year. One sees many a peasant with an income of about five or six hundred pounds sterling, who does not
disdain to till the soil that has enriched him. On it he lives a free
man.'

One finds, however, a somewhat less pedestrian interpretation of
liberty, as free discussion, on a later page: 'In England they do their
thinking in common, and letters are honoured more highly than in
France. This advantage is a necessary consequence of the form of
their government. There are in London about eight hundred persons who have the right to speak in public, and to uphold the
interests of the nation. About five or six thousand have pretensions
in their turn to the same honour. All the rest sit in judgement on
these persons, and anyone can have his thoughts on public affairs
printed: thus the whole nation is obliged to take instruction.'

There follows a pæan to commerce as the source of the greatness
of England. 'London was poor and rustic, when Edward III con-
quered half of France. It is solely because the English have taken to
commerce that London now surpasses Paris in the extent of the town
and the number of its citizens: that they can launch two hundred
men-of-war and hire kings as their allies.' He goes on to tell us that
an English merchant cherishes a proper pride, and compares

himself to a Roman citizen. He concludes with an invitation to the French bourgeois to think more highly of himself. Did his cudgelled shoulders ache as he wrote it? 'The (French) merchant is so used to hearing his occupation spoken of with contempt that he is stupid enough to blush for it. I am not sure, however, which is the more useful to the State, a powdered lord who knows precisely at what hour the King rises, and when he goes to bed, and gives himself great airs while he plays the part of slave in the waiting-room of a minister, or a merchant who enriches his country, gives from his office orders to Surat and Cairo, and makes his contribution to the world's well-being.'

Religion and politics occupy, however, barely a third of the book: the rest, after an entertaining account of English experiments in inoculation for smallpox, is devoted to science and literature. We need not consider here the illuminating and on the whole flattering account that Voltaire gives of English literature from his ultra-classical standpoint: to Pope goes the palm in poetry, and Shakespeare figures as a barbarian of genius. The French Academy is gently scourged, and England, in the honour she pays to intellect, is exhibited as a model to be imitated. Newton's national funeral deeply impressed his imagination.

Already Voltaire has started his life-work of transmuting the world's scales of value in accordance with liberal principles. Newton, he assures us, is the greatest man that ten centuries have produced. 'We owe reverence to him who conquers our minds by the force of truth, not to those who enslave men by violence, to him who knows the universe, rather than to those who disfigure it.' In six chapters, lightly and popularly written, and enlivened with his customary sallies of wit, starting with Bacon and proceeding through Locke to Newton, he gives an account of the intellectual revolution that in England had marched parallel with social and religious change. This was the first summary to reach French readers of the empirical philosophy and the new physics. Within its scope it is admirably done. Voltaire made no original contribution either to philosophy or to physical science, but he had the gift that Newton wholly lacked, of lucid and stimulating presentation. Thanks to him this achievement, the solidest part of the foundation of the modern belief in a rational universe, soon became the common possession of European culture—for French was in this century the universal language of the educated classes. What he did in these *Letters* was a mere preface. His complete statement of the Newtonian system, a book as full and accurate as it is readable, came later. Here he prepares his readers by a curiously contemptuous glance at Greek philosophy (of which, in truth, he knew little), some joking references to the schoolmen, and a not too respectful estimate of the Cartesian system, for an approach to the English thinkers. It was dangerous ground. Descartes in his lifetime was driven to seek refuge in Holland, but the Church had since contrived to assimilate his teaching and it was now for the learned and ecclesiastical world of France the one orthodox, the one tolerated scientific system. Voltaire has to apologize for these modest disturbers of intellectual peace. Locke's cautious empiricism—he describes him, elsewhere, tapping his way through the universe like a blind man with his stick—had indeed startled the orthodox, even in England. 'The superstitious are in society what cowards are in any army: they feel panic terrors and spread them.' 'Theologians are always ready to announce that God has been outraged, when one is not of their opinion.' After this characteristic clearing of the ground, there follows a spirited statement of Newton's theory of attraction, his optics, and his reform of chronology, with a much slighter reference to the infinitesimal calculus—a fairly heavy charge of intellectual dynamite to pack into a little book. Slight as it was, it must have given to countless readers their first glimpse of a new society and a systematic universe. Its publication made, as Condorcet tells us, a revolutionary epoch.

The five years that followed Voltaire's return from England were productive and eventful. Three new tragedies were staged, and the last of them, *Zaïre* (an echo of *Othello*), was as successful as his *Œdipe*, but it roused the orthodox, who found it theologically unsound. His verses on the death of Adrienne Lecouvreur infuriated the Ministry, as well they might, for there is in them the fire of a noble indignation. He had loved this lady, and followed her body when it was laid in unhallowed ground, for the Church still forbade the last rites of religion to any actor, however great. The English,

he tells his countrymen, laid Anne Oldfield with Newton and
Addison in Westminster Abbey. One may translate a fragment of
this poem thus:

> Rival of Athens, London, blest indeed
>   That with thy tyrants hadst the wit to chase
> The prejudices civil factions breed.
>   Men speak their thoughts and worth can win its place,
> Where art brings honour to a burgher's name.
>   He who at Blenheim brought Tallard to shame,
> The lofty Dryden and wise Addison,
>   Oldfield the charmer and Newton
> Share thy temple of fame.
>   In London Lecouvreur had found her grave
> Among the wise, the princes and the brave.
>   In London, who has talent he is great.

The publication of a much earlier poem, the *Epistle to Urania*,
caused the Archbishop of Paris to lodge a formal complaint with
the police. His *Temple of Taste*, a brilliant critical work, in the manner of the *Dunciad*, half verse, half prose, roused furious controversies with the elder Rousseau and his school. Paris split into furious
factions over everything he produced, and parodies of *Zaïre* and
the *Temple* were played on the stage. His *History of Charles XII*
was banned for dynastic reasons, and he was driven to print it
surreptitiously at Rouen. His 'boot-legging' Norman publisher
now produced (1734) without his consent his *Philosophical Letters*
on England, for he was not yet ready to issue this carefully meditated challenge.

Official France reacted promptly. Cardinal Fleury's amusement
had been short-lived. His lodging was searched and his papers and
money seized. The book was confiscated and condemned by the
Courts. On June 10th, 1734, it was publicly burned, as a 'scanda-
lous work, contrary to religion and morals and to the respect due to
the powers that be'. A sealed letter (*lettre de cachet*) ordered him to
be conveyed to the castle of Auxonne, a gloomy prison near Dijon.
Warned by his friend d'Argental, he fled in time from Paris.

III

HERMIT AND COURTIER

Voltaire's flight from Paris brings us to the period in his long career that finally shaped his destiny. His stay in England had made him what that age called a 'philosopher'. The libertines of the Temple were free-thinkers, who claimed, in private, licence for themselves, but they had no ambition to transform society, nor did they wage an open war on the Church from which most of them drew their livelihood. A 'philosopher' was in his outlook no less critical of the world around him, and no less sceptical in his attitude towards authority and tradition. But he was also positive and constructive, as the libertines were not. The basis of his rationalism was an enthusiasm for physical science, and with this was closely linked an ardent love of humanity, a 'philanthropy' which believed that liberty and science were destined together to bring an incredible amendment to human affairs. In the dazzling light of this imagined future he could dare to see the present as it was—the physical misery of the masses, the oppressions, the cruelties and the wars. This 'philosopher' incarnated in Voltaire's person must, however, fling off two forms of optimism that might cloud his vision of reality—firstly the naive complacency of a successful young man moving in a wealthy and luxurious society, and then the theoretical doctrine that Leibnitz formulated and Pope popularized. Using by turns persuasion, flattery and satire in his efforts to impose the liberal philosophy on the rulers of his world, it is only gradually that he will come to realize that he is engaged in a war of extermination in which there can be no quarter. Throughout this period of middle life he has no clear perception of his own place in this world. This brilliant, many-sided man is equipped for so many parts. He is witty, graceful, a brilliant talker; he could shine at Court and dazzle all Paris with his plays. He might win, as Prior and Addison did, some dignified political post, preferably as ambassador. Yet he is by his opinions, and also by his middle-class origin, the natural leader of an implacable Opposition. We shall see him, through twenty years, hesitating and compromising as he steers with futile cleverness a zigzag course. Always it is some accident that seems to deflect him from the path of worldly success, but always his own character, sure of itself and irrepressible in its militancy, was his destiny.

About this time a new influence entered Voltaire's life and dominated him through sixteen years. During the summer of 1733 he fell in love with the most remarkable woman of this age, Emily, Marquise du Châtelet. She had a powerful intellect, which she cultivated with a rare industry, and in this frivolous society she dared to be eccentric by her ardent study of the severer sciences. At 16 she had translated Vergil, but as her mind matured she lost her interest in poetry and even came to despise it. She would sit up all night, with her telescope, star-gazing; she aspired to original discovery in physics, and prepared herself by the study of mathematics for her translation of Newton's *Principia*. This 'blue-stocking' was, none the less, a passionately emotional woman. Men found her beautiful; women had to concede that she was attractive. Tall and sturdily built, she would sometimes dress with great magnificence, but in working hours she went about with ink-stained fingers in an old black apron. She loved music and had a beautiful singing voice. This brilliant woman had been married early to a commonplace soldier and country squire. She bore the Marquis three children, and then, her duty done, went her own way after the fashion of the times. It was a turbulent way, for this great lady did nothing by halves. She loved passionately and claimed the exclusive devotion of her admirers, with an exacting and possessive jealousy. Richelieu had come and gone in her affections before her intimacy with Voltaire began. A passionate lover he probably never was, but a more constant, devoted and affectionate friend she could hardly have found. Through sixteen years they were inseparable. They lived together like a married pair, but above all they worked together at physics and history, and played together in their private theatre. How he influenced her is obvious enough: he introduced her to Newton and English 'philosophy'. How she influenced him one can only guess, for their voluminous correspondence was burned after her death. Certainly she did not turn him from poetry, nor yet from history, for which she had no taste. Yet hers was not the weaker character of the two. She was, indeed, at times imperious. She had her full share of aristocratic pride, and unlike Voltaire, she found it difficult to realize that servants and the 'lower classes' were human. What Voltaire gained from her may have been a certain steadying in his purposes, an increasing concentration upon the bigger of the many tasks for which his versatile genius fitted him.

After a visit to the French army in Flanders, which feasted him in his disgrace, Voltaire went to the mansion of the Du Châtelet family, at Cirey in Champagne, and here while Madame lived, he made his permanent home. The family was poor and the house dilapidated. Voltaire was already a rich man, and throughout his long life his fortune grew. He made it easily, by speculating in grain and in lottery issues, and latterly as the sleeping partner of an army contractor. He collected pictures, among them a Titian and a Teniers. He had a keen interest in all the graphic arts, but especially in painting, though his taste had the limitations usual in the complacent classicism of this period. Gothic art he dismisssed as barbarism, and classed Velazquez among the second rate. He helped to furnish Cirey with considerable elegance, and hung its walls with Watteaus. In music his interest was less lively and it is barely mentioned in his history of civilization. Though he thrice collaborated with Rameau, and treated that difficult, bearish personality with friendly generosity, he thought his music tedious and pedantic. Familiar though he was with Germany, there is no sign that its music touched him, and in a list of the modern Germans who made a contribution to European culture, he mentions neither Handel nor Bach. This is not a little strange, for his must have been an aural rather than a visual mind. The grace and rhythm of his prose suggest it, no less than the easy movement of his verse, and this must be the explanation of his eccentric spelling: to proper names, more especially English names, he boldly gave a phonetic rendering. Evidently he had in his mind no visual picture of the map of Europe, for in a passage in his *Charles XII* he follows Shakespeare in giving a sea-coast to Bohemia.

From the letters of visitors to Cirey it is possible to reconstruct the life of these industrious hermits in their luxurious monastery. It was a lonely place, served by execrable roads. Voltaire and Madame rose betimes and worked in their own rooms till the early luncheon. She, indeed, was capable of working most of the night, with only two or three hours for sleep. After lunch, from 10.30 to 11.30, according to a precise ritual, there was an interval for talk in the lobby of Voltaire's study: at the end of half an hour exactly he would bow, and the company rose. The two hosts then returned to work till suppertime at nine. Guests were expected to amuse themselves, and if Voltaire visited them in their rooms, he never sat down, for he was greedy of time. There was, we are told, no easy-chair in his study. At meals, however, and especially after supper, he became gay and expansive. He treated the Marquise with courtly politeness and grace, though they quarrelled occasionally, but always in English, a language which they found congenial for this purpose. In company Voltaire talked brilliantly and lightly, and never lectured. Madame rode daily, and he would go for solitary walks in the woods, carrying a gun, though it is not recorded that he ever shot anything. If the Marquis was at home, he obligingly went to sleep during supper, and rose when served. There were, however, gala days in this otherwise sober existence. A small but beautiful theatre had been arranged, and here guests, neighbours and hosts would sometimes act as many as three plays in a day. Musicians were occasionally brought from the nearest town, and Madame would sing an opera.

The work this man did at Cirey was prodigious in quantity. From his youth he had been an enthusiastic letter-writer. In his early years his motive in writing was simply the wish of an expansive and affectionate nature to keep in touch with friends. Later in life he is the propagandist, expounding and discussing his liberal 'philosophy', who crushes opponents with a phrase, or mobilizes friends for a common effort. Letters in this century supplied the place of an uncensored press, and as Voltaire came to enjoy a European fame, his letters were passed round in copies, read aloud in drawing-rooms, and even reproduced in foreign newspapers. A modern writer can achieve the same effects with infinitely less labour, but

Voltaire's incredible industry went far, as one decade followed another, to defeat the censors. Where letters did not penetrate a, smuggled anonymous pamphlet in prose or verse, which bore his signature only in its inimitable style, would do his work for him. As his absences from Paris grew more continuous, so did the volume of his correspondence swell. At Cirey it is recorded that on one day he wrote thirty letters, which may have been an exceptional effort, and of these only two have been preserved. In grace, wit and spontaneous ease the best of his letters have never been equalled. They reveal, moreover, a man whose merciless militancy towards opponents was balanced by a warm and unrestrained affection for friends. His flattery of the great might revolt us, were it not for the art with which he performs even this exercise. But in truth a delicate courtesy was habitual to him, and when he wrote to an obscure person or to an intimate friend it obviously sprang from genuine feeling. Was ever a letter penned so graceful, gallant and kind-hearted as that which he wrote to a little actress of fifteen (Mlle Dangeville) who had spoiled one of his plays (*Brutus*) by her nervousness on the first night? Two early letters to Helvétius as a young man are perfect examples of mingled encouragement and helpful criticism. Nor did the art of being brilliantly generous desert him in old age. He tells his colleague and disciple Diderot, that on the arrival of a letter from him, he felt like some old, scarred veteran receiving a dispatch from Marshal Turenne. Was there ever a neater compliment to a soldier than the conclusion of his letter to Marshal Schullenbourg, 'with sincere wishes for the preservation of a life of which you have so often been prodigal'. If the most delightful and revealing of these letters are those to his 'guardian angels', his school friend d'Argental and his wife, which run to the end of his life, one respects him no less in the brief business-like notes to the Huguenot merchants and pastors who worked with him during the Calas affair. They are as nearly dull as Voltaire could be, for his tact forbids him to jest with these grave men, and yet they reveal the depth and sincerity of his feeling. It was difficult for this artist to touch paper without imprinting his personality upon it.

In addition to these letters, Voltaire, at Cirey or elsewhere, was nearly always at work on a tragedy: two of the most famous belong to this period, *Mérope* and *Mahomed*, but he wrote many more. Of his popular exposition of Newton we have already spoken. His chief occupation was, however, his two great histories, *The Century of Louis XIV* and the history of civilization (*Essay on Customs*). Of the latter he wrote only an early draft at Cirey, but the immense labour of collecting materials was done in close association with Madame du Châtelet. During some of these years these two, working in an improvised laboratory, hoped to make an original contribution to physics. Each, unknown to the other, competed for a prize offered by the Academy of Sciences for an essay on 'the propagation of fire'. Neither won it, but it went to a worthy victor, Euler, and possibly their Newtonian principles prejudiced the Cartesian Academy against them. Both, as competent judges have argued, showed originality: Voltaire, indeed, was on the verge of the discovery of oxygen, but just failed to make it. In his enthusiasm for science Voltaire recalls the universal genius of the next century, Goethe.

Early in the Cirey period there began the connection with Frederick of Prussia which coloured the whole middle period of Voltaire's life. Frederick, too, was a 'philosopher'. This bold freethinker and apostle of tolerance was also a student of literature, and until events made him a soldier, his chief ambition was to shine as a writer of French verse. It was natural that he should look on Voltaire as his master and his model. He began, before he reached the throne, to tempt him with offers of hospitality, couched in language that doubtless was at bottom sincere, in spite of its exaggeration. Not content with letters, he sent to Cirey an envoy, Baron Kaiserling, who brought with him the gift of a magnificent cane with a gold head of Socrates for handle. Madame's influence was from first to last against this connection. She had at this stage a good reason. Frederick as yet was merely the heir, and his father was an intolerant despot. Was it safe to put oneself in the old King's power? This was a temporary difficulty, however, whereas Madame's opposition was permanent, and it was not till after her death that Voltaire felt free to settle in Berlin. One is not sure what her reasons were. Her intuition may have warned her that a too close association with this royal egoist would end in disaster.

Frederick's attitude to herself was not helpful, for while he would use the conventional language of gallantry in writing about her, and was compelled to include her grudgingly in one of his many invitations, he too obviously had no wish to meet her. King and mistress were competing for Voltaire's person with an amusing jealousy, and while she lived he was loyal to her. When in 1742 Frederick offered him land and a house in Berlin, he replied that he preferred the second floor in Madame's château. She was miserable, however, during his visits to Germany, and evidently regarded them as minor infidelities. Her reply was to use her influence and skill to win recognition for him at Versailles. He should shine, not as an exile at a foreign Court, but as the brightest jewel in the French crown. The drama of his life throughout these years was a complicated triangular duel between this foreign king who courted him, his own sovereign who repelled him, and the woman whose pride it was to make him famous at home.

To turn Voltaire into a respectable celebrity was not an easy task. Thrice after the formal ending of his sentence of exile, he returned to Paris, and thrice he had to flee lest worse should befall him. Nothing would stop him from writing for the eyes of friends poems that were an offence to the respectable; nothing would stop his friends from circulating copies broadcast; when in due course they reached his enemies, he was forced too late to recollect that in their pockets lay the keys of the Bastille. A harmless, if not very elevated poem *The Man of Fashion* (*Le Mondain*) infuriated the devout. A far worse danger than this seemed to be impending, though in fact public discovery was delayed for many a year. Voltaire was writing his mock-heroic poem, *The Maid* (*La Pucelle*), and canto by canto it circulated among his friends, who shivered uneasily while they laughed. It was his favourite poem, his proudest achievement, and he was torn between an itch to enjoy the laughter that it caused, and terror lest it should be stolen and published, as eventually it was. It is certainly the most audacious work of its kind. There is no harm in choosing Don Juan as a subject for such a poem: that hero can be duly honoured in no other style. But it was reckless to laugh impartially at the national heroine of France and the Church that burned her alive. The poem has all the merits that one would expect from its author. The lines with their triple rhymes run with that effortless ease which led D'Alembert to compare Voltaire's versification to the Apollo Belvedere, 'athletic, noble, and at his ease'. Witty phrases and absurd inventions follow one another in prodigal profusion. Saints, monks, noble warriors, with the king and even the sacred Joan herself, dance indecorously through this riotous saturnalia. It is triumphant escape from all the trammels and conventions of reality, with this added spice, that its absurdities are apt to have that just perceptible resemblance to fact that makes satire. Critics of the last century, John Morley among them, found its licence unspeakably shocking. That, surely, is to bring morals into a world where there is neither sin nor virtue. These naughty deeds were never done by human beings, neither in Joan's century nor Voltaire's. They are the peccadilloes of phantoms that dance to triple rhymes. Verse has this magic, that it will lift him who submits to it beyond morals and probability. A rationalist might as well object to the mock-miracles as to the mock-sins. A sounder criticism of this long poem is that it is monotonous: one should not read more than one of its twenty-one cantos at a sitting. Byron knew better how to vary his matter and his mood. There is, when for a moment the laughter stops, a beauty in *Don Juan* and a depth of feeling that make it an incomparably greater poem than *The Maid*.

Voltaire knew, however, how to turn even danger to account. Once he fled to Holland and twice to Brussels. His fame migrated with him, and he gained a knowledge of many parts of Europe, which was of use to him in his histories. The third of these occasions was not a little mysterious. Two chapters of his *Louis XIV*, which had appeared in a miscellany, were seized and destroyed: as one reads them today they seem to be the work of a great patriot, who erred on the side of indulgence towards the monarchy. But the other King was now (1740) on his throne, writing letters to his master in which he begged him to address him simply as a man. Voltaire invented for him the too flattering title 'Your Humanity'. In September of this year they met for the first time at Cleves. The spell was not broken: they were in fact enchanted with one another, and Frederick wrote descriptions in which he praised the 'eloquence, the gentleness and the wisdom' of Voltaire. Two brief visits followed at short intervals, to Remusburg near Berlin and to Aix-la-Chapelle, as happy as the first. It had now occurred to Cardinal Fleury that Voltaire's credit at the Prussian Court might be used for diplomatic ends. He set out with the sanction of the French government, and on his return made quasi-official reports on his conversations with His Humanity. It was a somewhat equivocal part that he had to play, for France and Prussia were at war. Frederick, whose ambition it was to 'depopulate France of her great men', played a nasty trick to injure him at Versailles and force him to emigrate. He caused an excessively indiscreet letter of his to be circulated in Paris. On a second occasion, Frederick sent direct to Bishop Boyer, at this time an influential Minister, some verses in which Voltaire had laughed at this pompous personage. This philosopher-king was capable of every crime save stupidity. And in fact Voltaire was not thriving in Paris, though his tragedy, *Mérope*, had just been produced with an intoxicating success. Fleury had just died (1743) and Voltaire was a candidate for his seat in the Academy. Doubtless a pardonable vanity entered into his ardent wish for this honour, but his chief reason was a desire for security. The forty Immortals were rarely tenants of the Bastille. To achieve his end, he took, as his custom was, the shortest road. Finding that his reputation for impiety stood in his way, he addressed to this same Boyer a letter in which he had the meanness to write: 'I declare before God, who hears me, that I am a good citizen and a true Catholic', and went on to deny his authorship of the letters on England. Peter's cock must have crowed that night. This was the basest action of Voltaire's life, but it failed to open the Academy's doors. Rejected in Paris, he turned to Berlin and made a stay of four months in Germany. Socially it was a brilliant success. Balls, concerts, carnivals and operas were arranged in his honour, and the Prussian royal family acted his tragedies. He was, if possible, even more popular at the Court of Frederick's sister at Bayreuth. To the youngest of the royal sisters, his favourite, he wrote one of the most exquisite madrigals in the French language. The visit, however, had been undertaken with a serious diplomatic purpose, and in this Voltaire failed. He could not detach Frederick from his

allies, for the good reason that this shrewd prince felt more respect
for French poets than for French generals.

Very suddenly, very cheaply, soon after his return from Germany, Voltaire won at the French Court, with a trifle, the favour
that none of his solid work had brought him. The Dauphin was
about to be married, and for the festivities he condescended to
write the libretto of a ballet, *The Princess of Navarre*, for which
Rameau composed the music. It pleased Versailles, and the King,
a dull, pious man who loathed Voltaire, was induced to make him a
gentleman-in-waiting, to bestow a pension on him, and finally to
appoint him Historiographer to His Majesty. He did his duty by
writing a long poem on the French victory at Fontenoy. A second
ballet, *The Temple of Glory*, followed, again in partnership with
Rameau, to celebrate the victories in Flanders. In this Trajan was
the hero, and Voltaire, who could not wholly cease to be a philosopher when he became a gentleman, drew the edifying moral that
this conqueror repaid the ravages of war by constructive humanity.
It is said that he ventured, after the ballet, to seek the King's verdict,
by asking him with flattering bluntness: 'Is Trajan pleased?' Louis,
who never knew what to say, even in such a minor emergency as
this, turned his back without a word.

Again (1746) there was a vacancy in the Academy. On this
occasion Voltaire devised a more amusing way of silencing his pious
enemies. His play *Mahomed* (produced in 1742) had been well received. It is a powerful melodrama, with some passages of a moving
pathos, though the modern reader finds it hard to forgive the crude
portrait of the Prophet as a perfectly conscious deceiver. The
devout were suspicious. Was it not a covert attack upon the
Church? As a learned doctor of the Sorbonne pointed out, there are
the same number of syllables in the names of Mahomed and Jesus
Christ. Cardinal Fleury had obliged Voltaire to withdraw it after
the third performance. In preparing it for publication, Voltaire had
the exquisitely humorous inspiration of dedicating it to the Pope.
With a couple of Latin verses, some wire-pulling and a letter of
delicate flattery, the thing was done. Benedict XIV bestowed on the
author, with a medal, his apostolic benediction. 'Covered by the

stole of the Vicar of God', he marched triumphantly into the Academy.

This garment was, however, an insufficient protection. All that was pious and conservative in Paris broke into rage. It rained pamphlets and libels on the new Academician. One is not disposed to relate Voltaire's literary quarrels in detail. His contemporaries found them exciting: to us the very names of Desfontaines, Fréron and La Beaumelle become a weariness. They will live, if nowhere else, in one of his epigrams, provoked by a polemical book in which Fréron and La Beaumelle collaborated. On the title page stood a portrait of Voltaire, between engravings of his two assailants. One may translate it thus:

> Printers placed Voltaire's thin phiz
> Fréron and Beaumelle between.
> Were there but a good thief, this
> Truly Calvary had been.

None of his foes was worthy of his rapier, though Fréron was an able conservative journalist. Alike in the lawsuits into which Voltaire rushed, and in these verbal duels he pitifully sacrificed his dignity. There is this to be said for him, that he was never the aggressor, nor was there a good man among his victims. Desfontaines was an ex-Jesuit who had been imprisoned on a charge of homosexuality. This abnormality was punishable by burning alive, a penalty which another Jesuit had lately suffered. Voltaire, from pure humanity, rescued Desfontaines, a stranger to him, from the Bastille. With startling ingratitude this man then used his journalistic talents to destroy his benefactor. La Beaumelle was nothing but a specious literary pirate. None the less, Voltaire when roused to anger in a private quarrel makes an unpleasant spectacle. On this occasion he insisted, albeit after a fair trail, on the imprisonment not only of the minor poet and musician, one Travenol, chiefly to blame for the organized circulation of some odious printed libels, but of his aged father also.

At court, fortunately for mankind, luck was against Voltaire. Playing recklessly one evening at the Queen's table at Fontainebleau, Madame du Châtelet lost 84,000 francs. 'Come away,'

Voltaire said to her in English, 'you're playing with cheats'. It chanced that one of the company understood our language, and soon this treasonable accusation (not at that period improbable) was the talk of the Court. Voltaire fled precipitately (November, 1747) and found a refuge in the castle of the Duchess of Maine at Sceaux. Here, in a room in an isolated wing, with candles burning behind closed shutters, he lay hidden for two months. His only distraction was a nightly visit to the room of the old Duchess. She told him stories of Louis XIV's Court: he read aloud what he had written during the day. Behind the shutters he was composing *Zadig*, the best of his early tales in prose. Some of the matter of this fantastic Oriental romance was borrowed from Thomas Parnell—it was not an unmixed misfortune to know English— but into it Voltaire poured not a little of himself, and therefore this trifle will live for ever. As he wrote this narrative of the misfortunes that befell a philosopher of the Court of Bagdad, he was himself listening for the hoofs of the horses that might bring a royal 'sealed letter'. But that was not all. Easily, with jests and the charm of a born narrator, he worked into this tale some of his most cherished doctrines. The reader, hardly aware that he has read anything more than a whimsical romance, will put down the book imbued with the principles of toleration and the outlines of natural religion. What, apart from this, the conclusion of this edifying romance may be, it is not easy to say. The angel who enlightens Zadig expounds a rather virulent form of Leibnitzian optimism. The moral seems to lie in Zadig's monosyllabic comment: 'But . . .' This tale was worth the alarm in which it was conceived. Voltaire, in his shuttered refuge, found the technique that served him in many a later masterpiece.

Voltaire was not easily discouraged, and once more his pen opened the palace gates to him, and then closed them for ever. Madame de Pompadour, the King's acknowledged mistress, was among his admirers and herself acted in his new play, *The Prodigal Son*. He addressed some complimentary verses to her, in which he hinted, perhaps indiscreetly, at her empire over the King. It is not certain that he was actually banished for this offence, but in any event he left Court in disgrace. From Cirey, he and Madame went to Lunéville, where ex-King Stanislas of Poland kept his dwarf Court as Duke of Lorraine. Voltaire could charm any king save his own, and he was soon at his ease in this miniature Versailles. But a change had come about in his connection with Madame du Châtelet. The friendship of the two was unbroken and they still lived together in perfect intellectual comradeship, but he talked incessantly of his age and infirmities, and any physical relationship must have ended some time before the journey to Lorraine.

At the Court of Lorraine, Madame fell in love with the Marquis de Saint-Lambert, a young officer of the guard. He was a man of intelligence and charm, handsome, witty, a poet of some celebrity and a consummate egoist. The affair was tempestuous and unhappy. When in the autumn of 1748 Voltaire accidentally discovered their relationship, he was for some hours furious, and contemplated a duel. As one of the King's gentleman he was now sufficiently respectable to be run through by a nobleman's sword. Madame, however, brought him quickly to a more reasonable frame of mind, and this unusual man, who was never tepid, then behaved as the devoted friend he was. No shadow of egoism or jealousy seemed to linger in his mind, and he even accepted Saint-Lambert as an intimate and addressed him in graceful verses. At fifty-four he cast himself for an old man's part, and played it with undiminished enjoyment for thirty years. Madame had need of a friend, for she was soon with child. After an unedifying comedy, that simple man, her nominal husband, was induced to acknowledge it. Many another woman in this unembarrassed society must have done the same thing, but the usual thing is not what one would have expected from Madame du Châtelet. She finished her Newton a few hours before the child was born, and died ten days later (September 10th, 1749). Voltaire was stricken with passionate grief, fell as he descended the staircase from her chamber, dashed his head in despair upon the pavement, and then gave way to a moment of rage against Saint-Lambert. 'It is not at all a mistress I have lost,' he wrote, 'I have lost the half of myself, a mind for whom mine was made, a friend of twenty years. . . . I loved her as the most tender father loves his daughter.' For a time he thought of shutting himself up in the Benedictine Monastery of Senones, which had a famous library, and then of settling in England. Actually he took a house in Paris. Here he would pace up and down his room through the night, and his servants heard him calling Emily's name. Eventually he saved himself by hard work. In less than a year the inevitable happened: he settled as Frederick's guest in Potsdam in July 1750.

IV

LIBERAL HISTORY

No exact measure is available to inform us how this industrious man spent his time during the long years of retirement at Cirey. It is certain, however, that the major part of it went to the study and writing of history. This absorbing interest began with his school days and lasted to the end of his octogenarian existence. One hesitates, however, to class Voltaire as a historian. He was an event. If he wrote history, it was because he meant to make it. He never thought of time as a closed treasury choked with finished happenings. He felt it as a dynamic stream of movement. He made only the slightest systematic contribution to a scientific interpretation of history. In that Montesquieu surpassed him immeasurably, limited though his analysis was. Condorcet, in the daring little sketch that he wrote, without the aid of books, while he hid from the guillotine, made the first brilliant attempt at an evolutionary view. Vico, though none of the French philosophers had ever heard of him, had already laid some foundations. Buckle and Karl Marx were to venture their decisive forward strides in the next century. None the less, Voltaire brought to history a vivid sense of the continuity of man's life in time. He tried, as few of his successors did until our own day, to see the story of mankind as a whole, with China, India, and even Japan prominent in the vast landscape. His chief contribution, however, was that he brought to history the modern conception of causation. History, before his day, meant one of two things. It was either an uncritical chronicle, in which gossip, portents and miracles were mingled with a crude record of dynastic and military events, or else it was an edifying attempt to guess the designs of Providence. Bossuet's pious masterpiece, his fragmentary Universal History, was the last notable effort in the latter vein. In it, a devout man of genius tried to restate the vision of the divine plan in history, much as Saint Augustine had sketched it with a few bold strokes in *The City of God*. So conceived, history cannot be a pattern of causes and effects: it is a record of the Creator's will. Voltaire, after the earlier successes of physical science, made in this field also that transition from speculation over final causes to the tracing of efficient causes, which marks the beginning of science. He was, to be sure, no lonely pioneer: in this, as in all else, he was the typical intellect of his century. He and Montesquieu, with no marked mutual sympathy, were at work on similar tasks at the same time. David Hume and Gibbon were his younger contemporaries. All of them aimed at a lay science of history in conscious reaction against Bossuet, the Jesuit Daniel and their kind. Historians of our own day, absorbed for the most part in the minute work of collecting and sifting their data and documents, are curiously reluctant to recognize Voltaire's distinction. They feel more sympathy with the patient hunters, some of them nameless monks, who were busy throughout this century in Paris and Vienna in gathering and editing the records of the Middle Ages. That was indispensable work, but such things are raw material: they are not the history that becomes a part of culture. In that sense, if we accept history as a branch both of science and literature, at once a record of civilization and a contribution to it, it is no exaggeration to say that Voltaire was the first historian of modern Europe. Certainly, there is nothing that lives, no book worthy of the name of history, nothing that survives as an item in general culture between his *Century of Louis XIV* and the last of the classical Romans—for Montesquieu's epoch-making works were rather essays in interpretation than histories.

(i) METHOD AND PURPOSE

Voltaire was not self-conscious about the scientific aspect of his work. He had, indeed, a high ideal of accuracy. He believed in truth when relating all save autobiographical events; on any tendency in himself to mendacity he set a strict time-limit and confined it to the practical needs of his own lifetime. A dead Jesuit or a buried Pope he never slandered. Violent partisan as he was, he made a creditable effort to be fair, even to the enemy, even to Rome, when he sat down to write history. But in history as in all else, he was a practical man. He was aware of the future, while he explored the past. The oddest thing about this far from scrupulous man is that he was, first of all and all the time, a moralist of genius. His tragedies were deliberate lessons in morals and manners. His tales, even the most fantastic of them, were didactic. In his histories, he was doing what Plutarch and other classical writers had done; he was drawing from the past a lesson for the present and the future. There were reasons in the circumstances of his time that made history the readiest vehicle for the inculcation of a liberal philosophy. In a free society the teachers and prophets, from Burke to Carlyle and H. G. Wells, write their unembarrassed criticisms on the trend of contemporary events. To do that was difficult under Louis XV, though Voltaire sometimes risked it. Where free debate over current policies is hampered, the natural substitute is to draw one's lessons from the past.

This Voltaire did, and in his earlier explanations of his purpose confessed it with an engaging simplicity. From his prefaces to *The History of Charles XII of Sweden,* his first essay, one might suppose that the chief business of a historian is to write about kings for kings, though few in fact are worth the trouble. 'Such is the wretched weakness of men, that they admire those who have done evil brilliantly.' He offers us his judgements on the characters of Charles XII and Peter the Great, 'the two most singular personalities who have appeared for more than twenty centuries'. This is, he thinks, 'the way to render history useful'. Charles, he concludes, would have been a great man, had he granted peace when Peter sought it: as it was, he was merely a great soldier. 'Assuredly,' he remarks, 'no king could read the life of Charles XII, without being cured of the folly of conquest.' He reminds princes and ministers that they 'owe a reckoning to the public for their actions. It is at this price that they buy their greatness. History is a witness, not a flatterer. The only way to oblige men to say good things about us is to do them'. All this is a very naïve way of claiming that history is the final voice of public opinion. A prince may escape contemporary criticism while he seems to prosper, but no Bastille can silence this posthumous verdict. More than one potentate, he wrote many years later, 'has shrunk from a wicked action, because it would

instantly be registered in the archives of the human mind'. Doubtless Voltaire did suppose that by his books he was moulding his
royal pupils, of whom Frederick and the Tsarina Catherine were the
chief; in the latter instance and in one or two others, he may in some
degree have done so. What he chiefly did, however, was to arm the
younger generation with new canons of criticism—canons that
ended, in France at least, by sweeping princes away.

This was a young man's first approach to history, that did credit
to the classical education his Jesuit professors had given him. It
had all the conventionality of youth. Madame du Châtelet's positive,
scientific mind helped him to reach a more modern and constructive view. She had refused, until she met him, to take any interest in history whatever. She wanted a history of human society,
but in the books then available she found only battles and fables. She
suspected the distortion of Christian prejudice in all they told her
about Islam and Mahomed. She was outraged that Bossuet should
have devoted three-quarters of his space to the Jews, a people insignificant for history, whatever they may be for theology. Above
all, she was revolted by the chaos of unsifted and unco-ordinated
facts, always wearisome and often incredible. To justify history to
his friend, Voltaire had to maintain that it could be what it certainly was not, as Bossuet and Daniel wrote it, a science. Since she
was weary of these narratives of dynastic wars, he conceived for her
benefit what was nothing less than a first attempt, however imperfect, at a history of civilization, or as he significantly describes it, a
history of the human mind. He would attempt to show 'by what
stages mankind, from the barbaric rusticity of former days, attained
the politeness of our own'. His purpose, in short, was now to write
the history of human progress. The conception, as was inevitable, was
coloured by the intellectualism of this century. 'Therefore one must
write the history of opinion. That alone would make this chaos of
events, factions, revolutions and crimes worthy the attention of
wise men.' But in this field, also, the critical moralist returns. If he
is now less concerned with the virtues and follies of kings, he will
judge opinions by their consequences for human welfare. 'History
so conceived will show us errors and prejudices succeeding one
another in turn and driving out truth and reason . . . till slowly men

learn to think.' His aim shall be 'to enable the reader to judge of the extinction, the rebirth and the progress of the human mind'. It will be seen that a long intellectual journey lay between the first of Voltaire's histories, his *Charles XII* written in England in 1728 and *The Essays on Customs* (if that be the best translation for *L'Essai sur les Mœurs et l'Esprit des Nations*), of which the first rough sketch made at Cirey dates from round about 1740, though the book was not published till 1756. *The Century of Louis XIV* came between these two; begun about 1735, it was published only in 1754.

The *Charles XII* is rightly entitled a history rather than a biography. Of the intimate, personal life of this austere devotee of honour and glory—if indeed he had any—Voltaire tells us little. What he gives us is a superb narrative of the doings of this King of Sweden, who terrorized Europe, trampled on Poland, made his puppet its king, flung again and again his few battalions of disciplined ironsides at Peter's untrained hordes, until by beating them he taught them at last how to use their numbers. It becomes the most amazing tragi-comedy, as it recounts the doings, during his stay in Turkey, of this crazy king, by turns the guest, the master and the prisoner of its Sultan. Even after this climax, the interest, amid the fantastic plots and adventures of the last years, does not flag. Voltaire, as even Samuel Johnson had to admit, had a genius for narrative, but only a clumsy story-teller could have spoiled this tale. There are scenes in it that Voltaire manages with consummate dramatic art. Though he had never been in Turkey, he divined with surprising accuracy the mind and manners of the Turkish pashas who had to chain up this human comet. And indeed, in the more sober and ambitious books that followed, Voltaire is always peculiarly happy when he can indulge us with a stirring narrative. It would be difficult within a short compass to improve on his account of the adventures of the Young Pretender, or on his story of Anson's voyage round the world. His account of the hard-won French victory at Fontenoy makes one of the few chapters of military history that stir lively feelings and can be read with unflagging attention. He will turn aside to entertain us with the comedy of King Theodore's escapades in Corsica. Of anecdotes, in the usual sense of the word, he is sparing. He 'doubted everything' as he said of himself, 'but especially anecdotes', and he will repeat nothing without good evidence. But a few priceless stories and repartees come successfully through his sieve. That most respectable of kings' mistresses, Madame de Maintenon, a lady with an unsurpassed gift for managing the great, at last secretly married Louis XIV in his old age. She endured with difficulty the boredom of domesticity at her fireside through the long evenings with the weary and pious monarch. She confessed to her brother that she wished she were dead. 'I suppose, then,' he answered, 'that you have a promise from God the Father that He'll marry you.' In his account of the Church during the Dark Ages Voltaire includes a marvellous collection of well-authenticated miracles. A certain monk was responsible for so many that his prior forbade him to perform any more. One day he saw a thatcher falling from the roof of a house. The monk caused him to remain suspended in mid-air, while he ran to ask permission of his Superior to commit yet one miracle more. He was duly admonished but got what he sought, hurried back, and brought the poor workman safely to earth.

If Voltaire knows how to make the most of a dramatic situation and how to tell a story, he is curiously deficient in the sense for character. What he tells us to explain the sublime insanity of Charles XII is perfunctory enough: it all lies on the surface of the narrative itself. Elsewhere he excuses himself from attempting character-sketches. It is, he says, a charlatan's game to invent descriptions of persons whom one did not personally know. But he knew everyone of any note in the reign of Louis XV, yet his sketches in the continuation that deals with it are even slighter and fewer than in the great *Century* itself. This is a disappointing reticence, for he spent much of his social leisure in gathering impressions from the survivors of Louis XIV's reign. That he made full use of such material is certain, but rather to unravel doubtful facts than to stock his mental museum of portraits. The truth is, however we interpret it, that Voltaire lacked any lively sense of character. This is evident enough both in his tragedies and in his tales. The tales, at least, have merits enough to balance this defect. It explains, however, why his few comedies are failures.

Voltaire was a young man of twenty-four when Charles XII was killed, and he saw a good deal of his minister, Baron Gortz. A modern historian in his place would have visited Sweden, Poland, Russia and Turkey in search of data. This Voltaire never thought of doing, nor did he know the language of any of these countries. That, given the current use of French and even of Latin, was a less serious handicap than it would be today. He had no official documents to work upon, but this may have been an advantage, for his *History of Peter the Great*, based on such materials, is by comparison a lifeless work. He contrived to collect ample first-hand material in the shape of unpublished memoranda and letters by minor actors in this drama. He got more of these as the years went on, and enriched his book as new editions were demanded. These persons included two colonels in the Swedish service, three civilians who intrigued for the hero, three French ambassadors who had to deal with him, a Saxon field-marshal who fought against him, his puppet King of Poland, a relative of Voltaire's who was first dragoman at the Sublime Porte, the old Duchess of Marlborough, and many others, valets as well as princes, whom he met and questioned in London, Paris and at the Polish Court in Lunéville. He prints an impressive tribute to his accuracy from King Stanislas. That he weighed evidence sceptically is evident enough both in this book and in his later works. He was sometimes badly informed about the physical conditions prevailing in distant countries, for he lacked that rare reconstructive imagination that Defoe, for example, possessed. Thus he will tell us that India has the climate ideally adapted to the human species, and that Canada is a valueless desert of ice, not worth colonizing. On the other hand, he grasped the psychology of Turks and Poles with an uncanny power of divination. He tells us that the Polish nobility 'sold their votes but rarely their affections', and laughs at the poor gentry who 'while they groom the horses of their masters, boast themselves the electors of kings and the destroyers of tyrants'. The sources on which he relied for his *Century of Louis XIV* are rather more difficult to trace, for it was not customary in his day to give references. A high proportion of them were oral. The care, however, that he took to trace the precise responsibilities of successive ministers is evident enough. The greater part of this book and its continuation rests undoubtedly on the contemporary evidence of well-placed actors and observers, sifted and collected with equal industry and insight. Voltaire rarely tells us on what books he relied for his facts in writing the *Essay on Customs*, but it is clear that he ransacked the whole range of materials then available, from the Church fathers down to the narratives of the Jesuit missionaries in China, and he drew as lavishly from histories in the English language as from sources in Latin and French.

Of three of his histories one need say little, for they contain no very notable contribution of his own. The *Annals of the Empire* is, as its title indicates, a compilation and little more. In his *History of Peter the Great* he had to rely on data supplied to him by Catherine II. The book is distressingly inferior to his *Charles XII*, though Peter's constructive genius interested Voltaire very much more than the military prowess of the Swedish conqueror. He struggles rather painfully to be objective in his account of Peter's politic cruelties, notably the murder of his son Alexis. Some little personal touches are amusing—the emphasis, for example, on Peter's enthusiasm for silk-manufacture, the historian's own hobby. The *History of the Parlement of Paris*, though intended for a polemical purpose, is a work of minute research, that rested in part on unpublished documents. Any influence it can have had on opinion ended with the Monarchy itself.

Voltaire's fame as a historian rests today chiefly on his *Louis XIV*. The *Essay* is incomparably the more original and powerful book of the two, as it is also by far the longer. It is franker and bolder, and contains much more of the author's uncensored thinking on dangerous topics. One may safely say that the whole of Voltaire is in it. Unfortunately the science of history has advanced so notably since it was written, that it is now a dated document, valuable chiefly as a vehicle for Voltaire's reflections. *Louis XIV*, on the other hand, is still an indispensable source for the study of a great epoch, and it is also one of the recognized classics of French literature. One has the sense that one is exploring, as one reads the forgotten *Essay*, whereas every educated Frenchman is supposed to have read the less dynamic book. In *Louis XIV* Voltaire was on his good behaviour, for it belongs to that wretched period of his life when he aspired to the favours of the Court. This is, however, only relatively true: it was Voltaire and not the Historiographer-Royal who wrote this book. He speaks his verdicts and his criticisms plainly enough, though had he written a few years later, it is probable that these passages would have been rather longer, and that they would have been phrased with less restraint. In spite of its moderation, this history could not be published in France. To a certain extent its author is still blinded by the glitter of the glorious reign. He drank in this legend at school, and though he paints the shadows so faithfully that the reader is by no means impressed by the glory, it evidently lingered in his own mind. Like the *Essay*, though on a small scale, this is an attempt to write the history of civilization, indeed a very bold attempt, when one recalls that it is the first effort of its kind. The greatness of this century lay, for Voltaire, not at all in the magnificence of the Court, or in the scale of Louis' perpetual wars, but in its intellectual and technical advance. It was the first century of 'philosophy', or as we should say of rationalism. If Voltaire deploys all his stately rhetoric to exalt its greatness in literature, science and the arts, his real reason for this rather complacent self-congratulation is that thereby he helped his readers to break finally with the preceding ages of darkness and superstition. This was the great century, because it began with the foundation of the Royal Society and culminated in the Encyclopaedia. All this side of the book is admirably and nobly done, and has its due proportion of space. The economic history, on the other hand, though it has some brief passages of startling insight, is much too slight. This pioneer saw the importance of economics, but lacked the training or the assistance to work out his own intuition adequately. In spite of his frequent polemics against historians who fill their books with the record of wars, he devotes too much of his own space to this subject, until, as he himself recognizes in the Continuation, it becomes wearisome. Needless to say, when he tells at length the story of the religious disputes of this century, he is always entertaining, witty and effective. It is, however, a deliberately external record. He lacked the imaginative sympathy indispensable to the greatest historian. Let us

concede that these theological squabbles between Jansenists and
Jesuits were petty enough, when viewed in the long perspective
of the history of our race: let us admit that these propositions about
the various species of Grace, phrased in a barbarous jargon, mean
nothing on the surface for a modern mind, as they meant nothing
for Voltaire. None the less, would not a finer analysis have shown us
how certain permanent characters of the human mind, certain
emotional or intellectual needs of our species were, within these
spider's webs of dogma and tradition, struggling and writhing for a
clear utterance, which they did occasionally find in a page of Pascal?
Voltaire is so hostile to fanatical believers of all creeds, that he even
fails to recognize how the insistence of Protestants on their right to
the private interpretation of the Scriptures forwarded the cause of
free thought. This unsympathetic aloofness to religious thought is
unfortunate in his *Louis XIV*, but it handicaps him much more
seriously in the *Essay*, when he has to deal with the Middle Ages,
the religious Orders, and the early reformers. He writes well about
the persecutions inflicted on these early heretics, but he has little
curiosity about their efforts to think. It is not that he is deliberately
unfair. On the contrary, his conscious intellect is struggling all the
time to be objective and honest. Thus he feels a certain partiality towards the Quakers, on account of their humanity, and it is not
surprising that he eulogizes their behaviour to the Indians in
Pennsylvania. But it is greatly to his credit that he writes with
almost equal enthusiasm about the Jesuit colony in Paraguay, and
singles out these two cases as the redeeming exceptions in the
ghastly chronicle of the dealings of white peoples with primitive
races. One must, apparently, treat his account of Paraguay in *Candide* as a joke. While the total effect of his incessant polemics against
the Jesuits is annihilating, he paid several tributes to their services to
literature, and he goes out of his way to acquit them of the charge
that Jansenists and Protestants brought against them—that they
intended to corrupt morals. Again, while the arch-enemy is always
for him the Papacy, he has some pleasant things to say about
contemporary and recent Popes. What is more remarkable, he
singles out, in the *Essay*, Adrian IV for a notable eulogy, and
describes Alexander III, on account of his efforts to end serfdom,

as the man of all men who best served humanity during the Middle Ages, indeed as their greatest man. Voltaire, whatever be his short-comings, does however, achieve the effect at which he aimed. Looking down the long vista of his perspective, all this passion of the Christian sects over meaningless dogmas seems not a little ridiculous. He compels us to stand like Emerson under the stars and say to ourselves, 'Why so hot, my little fellow?' This, among other good reasons, was why in the *Essay* he devoted so much space to India, China, Turkey and Japan. 'It would be useful for those who are obstinate in these disputes to cast their eyes over the general history of the world, for in observing so many nations, customs and different religions, one perceives how small a figure a Molinist or a Jansenist cuts on the earth. Then one blushes for one's heat on be-half of a party that loses itself in the crowd and in the immensity of things.'

(ii) THE HISTORY OF CIVILIZATION

The *Essay* (though few would accept this verdict) is, with *Candide*, the greatest of Voltaire's works. Regarded as history it hardly deserves that place. It is something more and less than history. It is a sustained, serried argument based upon history, a plea of humanity against intolerance, and indeed against super-natural religion. It is one of the mightiest efforts of persuasion ever attempted, a pamphlet in the sense that Milton's *Areopagitica* may bear that name, but a pamphlet raised by its style, its learning, and its noble passion for humanity to the level of great literature. This aspect of it shall be considered in a later chapter; it concerns us here rather as an attempt at universal history. In fact it professes to run only from Charlemagne to Louis XIII, but it has a lengthy introduction that covers pre-history and deals in a very cursory way with sacred history. Classical antiquity is oddly omitted, save for some chapters on Constantine, the rise of Christianity and the causes of the decline of the Roman Empire. Though intelligent men were beginning in this century to feel a lively curiosity about primitive peoples, the science of anthropology had not begun. With the great civilizations that preceded the Hellenic, our modern acquaintance dates only from Champollion's visit to Egypt as a member of Napoleon's staff. Voltaire's introduction is, therefore, a reminder that our own knowledge is very recent. Voltaire missed a chance or two of seeing farther than in fact he did into the remoter past. Buffon and some of his contemporaries were groping after a first glimpse of the theory of evolution. Voltaire, on the other hand, is quite sure that the various races of mankind are absolutely distinct, and in a letter he laughs at the 'impostors' who anticipated Darwin by guessing at 'that very remarkable epoch in which the brutes our ancestors developed into men'. He flatly rejects some of the strange tales in Herodotus which modern anthropology has rendered credible, notably his account of prostitution in the temple of Melitta at Babylon.

On the other hand, there are in this introduction some remarkable flashes of insight. Voltaire maintains, against Hobbes and his school, that man was not originally 'a wolf' to his fellows; there never was 'a state of nature' in the sense of a condition of brutish isolation and individualism. From the first, man was a social being, endowed with the virtues indispensable to life in a group, pity and a sentiment of justice. Again, Voltaire, arguing that if the Chaldeans started their astronomical reckonings in 2234 B.C. they must have had a fairly elaborate culture for many centuries before this date, anticipates our modern recognition of the immense antiquity of civilization. What is even more astonishing, he throws out the diffusionist theory as a brilliant guess. He notices the frequent occurrence all over the globe of baptism as a rite, and suggests that with all other rites it may have originated among the Persians or Chaldeans and spread to the ends of the earth. For the Egyptians, however, he entertained a deep contempt, only surpassed by his detestation of the Jews—though he pulls himself up to protest against anti-semitic persecutions.

Voltaire finds 'the thread that leads through the labyrinth of modern history in the long struggle between the secular and the clerical power'. This was for him a dangerous, because a welcome, discovery. It does in fact furnish an invaluable clue to much of the political history of Europe, from the creation of the Holy Roman Empire down to the Bull 'Unigenitus' in his own lifetime. But the more tempting it is as an international link of unity, the more does it tend to throw economic history into the shade. It is the perfect clue for an anti-clerical pamphlet, but it yields a defective pattern for a broad history of civilization. Amid the strife of Guelphs and Ghibellines, it leads on comfortably enough through the Crusades to the Reformation and the religious wars. But it tempts Voltaire, stressing the political aspect, to ignore the social and economic changes that made the environment of all these happenings. He devotes a fair amount of space to letters, science and the arts, yet rather less than his own conception of history should have prescribed. He apologizes for some inadequacy in this matter, due to the loss of a mass of manuscript material that he and Madame du Châtelet had collected to illustrate the progress of manufacture and the arts, and also of some verse translations from Arabic and Italian poets. What we get under these heads is rather slight, but there are some fine pages on Arabic civilization, and on the first triumphs of physical science. In general, Voltaire's treatment of the Middle Ages suffers from the contempt that his century felt for every manifestation of Gothic genius. Of the chapters on India and China, one cannot say more than they are well-meaning and spirited attempts to correct our European insolence. Too little was known as yet about their history, but his account of the Far East becomes instructive from the moment that Jesuits appear upon the scene. He was perfectly correct in his contention that up to the seventeenth century the civilization of the East equalled or surpassed that of Europe. He makes no secret of the reason for his enthusiastic partiality for the Chinese: their educated class, he was convinced, professed Deism. That was too elegant a simplification.

In this gallant attempt to weave history into a coherent whole, did Voltaire work out any system of interpretation? Systems were far from him: his was an empirical mind. But to some generalizations he does commit himself, as he goes along. They are not on a surface view altogether consistent, nor do they succeed in making conscious all the assumptions on which he habitually worked. He has, as we have seen, a faith in progress, but it is much less dogmatic than the system which the younger generation of 'philosophers', Helvétius, Condorcet and Godwin was to erect. In 'opinion',

backed sometimes by force, sometimes by fraud, he sees the sinister
force at work in history. By this word he seems to mean faulty
reasoning, and usually superstition, as opposed to sound reasoning
and 'philosophy'. It is the basis of certain institutions, the Papacy
for example, and the Caliphate, which will lose their ascendancy as
philosophy gains its empire over men's minds. So far he goes,
but no farther, for he does not explicitly argue as his followers did,
that men's minds are malleable stuff, entirely shaped by the institutions under which they live. He does, however, imply something
of the kind, with the reformer's comfortable corollary, that if
enlightened princes will but change these institutions, we may con-
fidently count on human improvement as a consequence. He is sure
that the decisive conditions of progress are under human control,
for he rejects Montesquieu's fatalistic emphasis on climate. If, he
argues, climate were the decisive factor, why was it that Christianity, originally an oriental religion, perished in its native climate of
Asia, and throve in Europe? The clearest enunciation of this progressive reasoning occurs in his rhymed letter to the Tsarina
Catherine II (1771) in which he incites her to conquer Turkey and
liberate the Greeks:

> Thine it shall be, great Queen, to change the meek
> And plant thy courage in the quailing Greek.
> It is not climate makes us what we are.
> Peter made men, but thou, divine in war,
> Shalt heroes fashion. Monarchs, by their grace,
> Can shape the mind and morals of our race.

This is, however, only the first rough draft of the doctrine of Per-
fectibility, and one suspects that Voltaire's common sense would
have laughed at the visions in which his disciples indulged, for they
held out hopes that reason would eventually vanquish those twin
infirmities, death and sleep. Such fantasies he ridiculed in Maupertuis.

The younger men who followed Voltaire were not historians—
indeed, Diderot in his conduct of the Encyclopaedia had such a
contempt for the past, that he neglected history as useless lumber.
Faced with the concrete facts of history, did Voltaire really suppose

that mankind has marched in step with syllogisms? Was it really better reasoning that led to the decay of superstitious 'opinions', and the triumph of 'philosophy'? Or shall we say that men's beliefs succeed each other as the effective shapers of history, according as economic changes favour the rise or fall of the class whose interest is served by a particular intellectual attitude? On this latter view, the decisive fact was not that science and philosophy undermined 'superstition' by hard reasoning between the genera-tions of Wicliffe and Newton. What happened was that a number of economic changes gave the middle class an advantage in its rivalry with the feudal class, linked as it was with the clergy; and that this middle class, to justify its own pretensions to power, was driven to oppose the whole fabric of authority, the divine right alike of kings and of popes, on which its opponents relied. The 'opinion' fell when the interests of a sufficiently powerful middle class required that it should fall. The fact is that Voltaire never seriously addressed his mind to this problem. His works are strewn with summary generali-zations which yield no coherent view of the mechanics of historical movement. 'Three things,' he tells us, 'exercise a constant influence on men's minds: climate, government, religion; this is the only way of solving the riddle of this world.' One notes here the omission of any mention of economic conditions, the organization of labour, the ways by which men gain their bread. If one inquires how changes come about in the two of these three factors that are variable, government and religion, his answers seem flatly contradictory. At times he relies absolutely on reason: 'God gave us reason ("un principe de raison universelle") as he gave feathers to birds and fur to bears. . . . In the end it always gets the better of tyrants and super-stitious impostors. . . . In the long run even the simplest people can judge what is for its good.' In another mood, however, he will say that 'force achieves everything in this world'. Sometimes he associates force and money. The Stuart cause finally failed, since this is an age, 'when military discipline, artillery and above all money decide everything in the long run'. There are other passages in which he seems to attribute all initiative in history to the genius of great men. Thus he tells us that 'Alfred the Great stands in the front rank of the heroes who have served the human race, which but for these extraordinary men would have resembled the wild beasts for ever'. Again in a passage about Henry the Navigator he writes: 'Rarely has anything great been done in this world save by the genius and firmness of one man, who struggles against the prejudices of the multitude, or imposes his prejudices upon it.' Elsewhere (notably in his *Louis XIV*) he throws out the suggestion that there is a natural rhythm or cycle in human development, so that a great efflorescence of talent is necessarily followed by a period of sterility. Creative and imaginative literature can flourish only for a century: thereafter comes the epoch of criticism.

One is forced, then, to abandon the attempt to draw from Voltaire any systematic interpretation of historical movement. But the more one reads of him, the more one is impressed by one assumption that returns again and again. He believes that men act primarily on economic motives, and to economic changes he does in fact ascribe the main trend of political and social evolution. He never enlarges on this opinion: he treats it as something self-evident, accepted by common sense, and yet in his rather meagre attempts to theorize, he forgets it altogether. In this way he interprets the Crusades in general, and particularly that directed against the Albigenses: 'its origin lay solely in the lust for other men's property.' In writing of the Reformation, he reminds us on every page that the Church was a vast mechanism for extracting money: 'relics, indulgences, dispensations, benefices, everything was sold.' The revolt of the Protestant middle class is interpreted primarily as the effort of an exploited population to free itself from a galling tribute to a foreign Power. The Gallicanism of the French Church is reduced to the same simple elements.

All this is naïve enough, and by no means peculiar to Voltaire. On occasion, however, this instinct for the economic interpretation of history leads him to some much more interesting bit of analysis. In the reflections with which he concludes his *Louis XIV* (Chapter 30) he traces the social consequences of the monetary inflation (though he does not use that word) which had been going on in France and in Europe generally through two centuries. The volume of currency had been increased so that the cost of living had more than doubled. Yet the salaries, pensions and pay of ministers, courtiers and soldiers, had remained unchanged. The infantry soldier still received his four sous, as in the time of Henri IV, though the real value of money had sunk to one third. If only 'these ignorant men who sell their lives so cheap' were to demand their due, armies throughout Europe would have to be cut to one third, and agriculture and industry would be the gainers. 'One must add that since the gains of commerce have increased, while the salaries of all great offices have diminished in real value, there is less wealth than formerly among the great, and more in the middle class, and this has lessened the distance between men. There was formerly no resource for the small man but to serve the great: today industry has opened a thousand roads that were unknown a century ago.'

That is all he has to say on this subject, yet in this brief but pregnant passage he has given us the ultimate explanation of the middle-class revolution. A number of external changes, of which monetary inflation was one, increased the economic power of the mercantile and industrial classes at the expense of the old feudal governing class. In the long run the contradiction between the political impotence of the middle class and its economic strength became too flagrant, and feudalism was swept aside. Implicit in this quiet page of Voltaire's is the essence of the Marxist interpretation of history, but it seems to him so obvious, so much a matter of daily experience, that he fails to perceive its theoretical interest. Lapses of this kind are not uncommon in the history of thought: theory is apt to lag behind experience. The result was that a whole generation of 'philosophers' lived in a haze of illusion, nor did this misfortune cease with their death. Theory told Voltaire to rely for progress on the good sense of mankind and on rational persuasion. Experience and history taught him that in fact slow economic changes, which may escape all human control, make the conditions that govern political movement. But he never tried to relate his optimistic faith in reason to his realistic perception of the all-importance of economic motives and forces. In short, he worked out no tactic for progress, nor did any progressive thinker attempt it in his generation or the next. This does mean that his superb work of persuasion was wasted. It was necessary in this way to give confidence and direction to the middle class, which already had the economic weight necessary for a decisive act of self-assertion. It was also useful to demoralize the old guard of a doomed order by rendering it odious and ridiculous. In these frontal attacks Voltaire's life was well spent. It is when he hopes everything from the arrival in office for a brief term of some well-meaning minister, or when he tries to use for the cause of reform the faintly liberal inclinations of a king's mistress, that one frowns, not without sympathy, at this waste of his time and talents. He failed, as all the liberal philosophers did, to face the crude issue of power. The old order would not reform itself till it was forced to yield. These crudities of history are always the last of the realities that sensitive and reasonable men can bring themselves to face.

(iii) THE NEW VALUES

Voltaire, as we have seen reason to suspect, was above all things a great moralist, who used history to convey a definite body of practical teaching. That, however, is to underestimate the subtlety of what he did. Sometimes by his comments on events, sometimes by his estimates of men, he was steadily changing the values of any mind that submitted itself to his influence. From the vast but orderly mass of concrete detail in these great histories there emerges something of greater significance than the marshalled facts—a sharply defined view of the ends that society should serve, criteria for judging the purposes and achievements of princes and ministers, a new vision of the goods after which a wise man will strive. With all its humanity, yet with its manifest limitations, the liberal view of life and society was fixed in these histories, thanks to the magic of their style, in a form so attractive and memorable that it became the decisive intellectual influence that moulded the progressive half of mankind for two or three generations to come. Those who preferred a brief essay, light, witty and confident, would find the same views restated in Voltaire's *Philosophic Dictionary*, and many who read little or nothing of Voltaire himself would still absorb his teaching from his disciples, the Condorcets, the Godwins, the innumerable journalists and pamphleteers who steeped themselves in his books.

What, then, was the content of Voltairian liberalism? The items of it that can be cramped into a definite programme are far from being its most vital part. It was an attitude to life, an emotional habit based on the choice of certain values and the rejection of others.

The precise articles of belief are none the less of the first importance. Chief among them comes toleration, freedom of thought and speech. Linked with this is the claim that the secular power in all the affairs of daily life on this earth shall be supreme over the ecclesiastical power. Of these basic demands we shall have more to say in a later chapter (IX). The political doctrine is clear enough in its general drift, but somewhat sketchy in detail. The time had not yet come to discuss the articles of a liberal constitution. Voltaire rarely goes beyond the plain settlement that what he wants in France, and elsewhere in the civilized world, is something like the British Constitution. Indeed, he says that unless it is adopted, revolution is inevitable. He applauded it in the *Letters on England*; defined it a little more closely in the big *Philosophic Dictionary*, and never tired of pointing to it, in poems, histories and letters, as the happiest model of government that mankind had worked out since the great days of Athens. Thought was free and talent was rewarded. He had an uneasy suspicion that corruption prevailed at Westminster, but this he stifled. He admired, with the Whigs, the English system of checks and balances. He could also admire, even with lyrical enthusiasm, 'democracy' as it existed in Switzerland. But he thought this system suitable only for small States, for he used the word in its original sense—government by assemblies of all the citizens. In this relative world of compromise he inclined to constitutional monarchy as the best expedient. In some passages of the *Essay*, he seems to express a positive enthusiasm, even a veneration for kings as such. The context shows, however, that he is here backing a king against a pope, and in such a cause Voltaire was not the man to stint a little exaggeration. Elsewhere, in a jocular mood, he explains that if he had to make the painful choice between monarchy and oligarchy, he would prefer one despot to many. But he will do his utmost to rob the monarch of arbitrary, personal power. He boldly argues that all monarchies were originally

C

elective. He always reminds us in discussing the dynastic arrange-
ments of this century, that the people of Spain or Silesia were never
consulted. But his case against the French monarchy of his day was
not so much that it retained no vestige of representative institutions,
as that it obeyed no impersonal system of law. He devotes, accordingly, much space in the histories to the sharpest criticism of the
arbitrary exercise of personal power by monarchs and ministers,
notably Cardinal Richelieu and Louis XIV. From this he goes on to
detailed criticism of the working of the legal system. He conducts
an unwearied guerrilla warfare against torture—the 'question' as it
was euphemistically called. Mordant phrases about it are scattered
all over his writings, but the passage that lives in the memory is an
imaginary description of the feelings of a young wife, when her
husband, the judge, first returns fresh from the 'question' to her
embraces. The crazy severity of punishments and the ghastly frequency of executions move him to horror. There are good pages
about the shocking system of interrogation, in which the accused
never confronted his accusers or their witnesses, and never enjoyed
the help of counsel. There are protests against the anti-social
practice of confiscating the estate of a convicted person, and much
more in the same vein. But one may sum up the whole of Voltaire's
political writing in a sentence. He demanded for himself and his
fellow-countrymen the same measure of political liberty that he had
enjoyed in England. More than that he did not claim. Had he lived
to see the Revolution, he would not have taken his seat on 'the
Mountain'.

Voltaire uses many methods in his constant endeavour to trans-
value, in a liberal sense, the values of his readers. The most effective
of his devices is to arrange the salient names of history in a new
order. He drags the mighty from their seats with cold, industrious
passion, and sets in their places the new heroes of humanity. It is the
conquerors whom he specially delights to depose. Constantine
emerges from a lengthy examination an abominable figure. Charlemagne fares, if possible, worse. The savagery of his conversion of
the Saxons to Christianity by force is told in sharp, visual detail:
'their idol was overthrown and their priests massacred upon its
fragments.' He goes on to describe the enslavement of these con-

verted German tribes, and the abominations of Vehmic justice. Nor
will he allow us to forget that the Church canonized this pious
butcher. No one else is handled quite so roughly, unless it be Louis
XI, the first Most-Christian King of France. Voltaire doubted his
own ability to sketch the character of distant personages, but he
paints a convincing portrait of the piety, the superstition, the
cruelty and the fears of this able despot, who debased the nation,
till it 'lay tranquil like convicts in the galleys', wore a medal of the
Madonna in his hat, and made her Countess of Boulogne. 'Piety,'
he comments, 'does not consist in making the Virgin a countess,
but in abstaining from actions that conscience condemns.' Still, he
did some good: he stopped the Parlement and the University
from 'persecuting as sorcerers the first printers who came from
Germany'. He is merciless to Richelieu, who 'achieved the unity of
France only that he might vex and divide her neighbours'. Mazarin
he dismisses in a phrase that Tacitus might have envied—he was
'guilty of all the good he did not do'. But perhaps the subtlest of his
performances is a formal comparison between Louis XIV and his
adversary William of Orange. It is done with scrupulous fairness:
none of Louis' glories is forgotten, while William's record is set
out in cool, unemotional words. Voltaire leaves us to judge—
because he is sure of his effect. Then was he, as is commonly said, a
purely destructive genius? On the contrary, he compiles, as he goes
along, his own calendar of saints. Some kings are in it, notably
Alfred the Great and Henri IV. He will even admit a Pope, Alexander III. There are ministers who have served the people well—
Sully, Colbert, Turgot. But it is on the thinkers, the scientists and
poets that he lavishes his titles of honour—Bacon, Tycho Brahe,
Kepler, Racine. Their names draw from him, again and again, a
glowing page of unrestrained eloquence. History, like the God of
the Deist creed, dispenses rewards as well as punishments. A Cromwell lives for a day, but Newton is immortal. Sometimes he will
canonize a perfectly obscure mortal, for no reason but that he served
his fellows well. Thus he devotes a page to a certain Comte d'Ennery,
an administrator who left his constructive works behind him in
colony after colony. 'He dug canals, while others devastated the
earth.'

One soon comes to perceive what Voltaire is doing in this
running commentary on the masters of human achievement. He is
suggesting to his readers the attitude that was afterwards labelled
Positivism, though his version of it had none of the pedantic
dogmatism of Comte's. Immortality beyond the grave he rejects.
We have but one life to lead here below. We cannot hope to
know ultimate truths. 'What really matters is that this poor species
of ours should be as little miserable as possible.' There is therefore
but one thing to applaud in history, a record of creative work. If he
admires Elizabeth of England and Henri IV it is because they
fostered commerce, industry, agriculture. That is why he is partial to
Colbert, though, like the physiocrats, he censures that able minister
for his failure to allow the free export of grain and freedom of
internal trade. He is sure that it is commerce that enriches a nation,
and he drives that moral home by proving that the riches of the
New World flowed eventually not to Madrid, which drew its tribute
from the gold-mines, but to London which traded with the Spanish
colonies. He was among the first to state the classical liberal conviction that commerce makes for peace. 'It is destined to be the
bond between nations, to console the earth, not to devastate it.' If
this be so, then it follows that the only title to honour is some form
of creative work. He therefore raises the trading and industrial
class to the first rank in society. He will pour contempt (as in the
Letters on England) upon an idle nobility, and he is even more
hostile to the monastic orders. This is the real basis, or at least the
moral justification, of his constant attacks on every form of class
privilege, but more especially the exemption in France of the
nobility and clergy from direct taxation. 'It is madness in a government to debase the greater part of a nation.' He can even forgive
Louis XI for his brutal and treacherous humiliation of the great:
'Fifty families murmured and more than half a million rejoiced.' He
is the typical Liberal in his enthusiasm for any State that will erect a
ladder by which merit of humble birth may rise to greatness.
'Merit could never in Venice raise a simple citizen. . . . The beauty of
the government of England . . . consists in this counterpoise, and
in the road ever open to honour for whoever is worthy of it.' He
greets the first signs of this readiness to promote humble talent in

the public service under Louis XIV. 'Citizens who formerly would have been proud to serve these nobles as their domestics, have become their equals and often their superiors in the military service. The more service of all kinds prevails over titles, the more does a State flourish.'

In all this one meets the rising middle class, at length, in the intellect of this man, perfectly articulate and fearless. This attitude to an idle, unproductive aristocracy is so familiar that one need not dwell on it, but one is more curious about his formulation of the middle-class view of the 'lower orders'. He will on occasion group together, against the nobility and the clergy, all the rest of 'the people, the most numerous, the most useful, and even the most virtuous part of mankind, composed of those who study law and science, the merchants, the artisans and lastly the labourers, who follow the first and most despised of occupations' (English Letter IX). In other passages he dwells on the degradation of the rustic population of his day, much inferior, he tells us, to the so-called savages of North America. He boldly affirms his sympathy, again and again, with the cause of the masses in the various peasant wars. 'The war of Spartacus for the slaves was the most just war in history, perhaps the only just war.' Of the Anabaptists, he writes: 'They stressed that dangerous truth which is in all our hearts, that men are born equal, and that if the popes treated princes as subjects, the gentry treated the peasants as beasts.' He approves their social programme: 'they claimed the rights of man, but upheld them like wild beasts'—a verdict he would doubtless have repeated in 1793. In an article in the *Philosophic Dictionary* (égalité) he wrestles in obvious distress with this problem of inequality. God gave us reason' (to summarize it in his own words) 'and the fruit of it is that man is enslaved over almost all the earth. . . . The real evil, however, is not inequality but dependence. It is inevitable that mankind should be divided into two classes with many subdivisions—the oppressors and the oppressed. Fortunately use and wont and the lack of leisure prevent most of the oppressed from realizing their condition. When they do feel it, there ensues civil war, which can end only in the enslavement of the people, for money is the sovereign power within a State. Equality is impossible, since men are born with a disposition to domineer, and with a taste for idleness. The race can subsist only if there be an infinite number of useful men who possess nothing at all. None the less one should not push inequality to extremes.' Complete freedom of migration, he now argues, is a partial solution. 'Labourers should be free to come and go. A well-governed country will keep its own and attract others. Those born to serve must learn to do their lowly duty, for otherwise all human society is perverted.' A briefer passage in *Louis XIV* conveys a similar conclusion: 'the labourer and the artisan must be cut down to necessaries, if they are to work: such is human nature. It is inevitable that the majority should be poor, but it is not necessary that it should be wretched.'

These passages in their frankness make a priceless contribution to honest thinking. The cynicism of the phrasing betrays Voltaire's uneasiness. He knows very well that the principles of the middle-class revolution, stated as they were with a bold universality, ought to lead to economic equality. But he sees as clearly that this would conflict with the interests of that class. He justifies himself by taking a view of human nature that he had rejected in another context. For he had told us that all society rests on the sentiments of pity and justice natural to man. Here he proclaims a fundamental egoism. He does not shrink from asserting that the sanction of any society based on inequality must be force, hired by economic power. He faces, as the English aristocracy that enclosed the commons frankly did, the necessity for reducing the masses to a proletarian level, in order that they shall work for the advantage of others. The only tinge of hypocrisy comes at the end, where he claims that all this must be done in the interest, not of 'the oppressors', but of society. With the suggestion that the mobility of labour will mitigate the hardships of inequality we are already in the nineteenth century, amid the economists who opposed the Factory Acts in the name of *laissez-faire*. None the less it is clear to anyone who knows Voltaire's habits of speech that he is in the grip of an uncongenial argument. What he states is the authentic middle-class doctrine: but it revolts his humanity.

Humanity in this dilemma might win in actual practice, as in Voltaire's own conduct it did, but it never wins in the battle of theory. Education furnished a test case in this century and the next. Unlike Condorcet and Turgot, Voltaire had no faith in universal schooling, even though this meant that the masses would remain sunk in superstition. Writing to D'Alembert in 1757, he says that he would 'deny education to labourers'. They would 'die of hunger before they became philosophers': education 'would spoil them for the plough. It is not the labourer who should be taught, but the good bourgeois, the townsman'. Ten years later, after nearer acquaintance with the watchmakers of Geneva, he concedes that artisans, but not labourers, should be instructed, for he found that the former were already reading. He sees the danger of ignorance: 'everything is lost when one treats the people as a flock of bulls, for sooner or later they gore.' At Ferney he maintained a free school for the workers' children.

This hesitating attitude to education is the more surprising since throughout his writings he magnifies the intellectual life. He means by it nothing exalted or remote, not the contemplative life (theoria) of Aristotle, and certainly not the mysticism and devotion of the contemplative Orders. He means something wholly concrete. the pursuit of the sciences, the arts, and the polite, cultured existence of a leisured class. To this last he attaches immense importance, though he will call it, when he recollects the cruelty of the age, 'a blood-stained robe of silk and gold'. To foster this spirit of society has been the peculiar glory of the French, and above all of French women, to whose civilizing influence he pays many a tribute. He was instinctively what we call a 'feminist', though he never worked out a programme of emancipation, as Condorcet so nobly did. It is latent, however, in a witty little trifle of his entitled, *Wives submit yourselves to your husbands*. In Voltaire's mind the triumphs of science are always in sharp conflict with the glories of war and the tinsel of royal magnificence. He rarely applauds scientists without exalting them above conquerors.

From this position he moves on insensibly to a cosmopolitan outlook. He prides himself on writing to English 'philosophers' while their countries are at war: there is a republic of letters above the battle: 'minds that think like yours are my countrymen and my friends.' The thought of national rivalry distresses him. 'Must a good patriot be the enemy of the rest of mankind? ... One country cannot gain without another losing, nor conquer without making others wretched. ... The citizen of the universe must be content that his country shall be neither greater nor less, neither richer nor poorer.' This is muddy thinking, at variance with his aphorism about commerce, the bond of unity, but the tendency is clear enough. It runs throughout his writings. He perpetually labours to correct the racial, religious or national arrogance of the society in which he found himself. He delights to dissipate Christian slanders or misunderstandings of Mahommedanism. He places the humane and chivalrous Saladin in his calendar of saints. He examines and rejects unpleasant tales about Tamerlane and Mahomed II. He insists that it was the high culture and the science of the Arabs of Spain that stimulated the revival of learning in Europe, rather than the influence of the Byzantine Greeks. He never tires of contrasting the English and the French, always to the disadvantage of his own countrymen—save, indeed, in the theatre. He dwells on all the good that can fairly be said of the more notable enemies of France, our own Edward III, who behaved at Calais with true humanity, Pope Julius II, and, above all, William of Orange. This trait in him is more than perversity and love of paradox. It springs from a rooted distrust of nationalism, a love of humanity as one great family.

It is, however, in his attitude to war that Voltaire reveals most clearly his cosmopolitanism, his rejection of nationalism. It is not that he is insensible to the splendour of physical courage: indeed, he delights to tell anecdotes of French bravery on the battle-field, more especially if the hero were an abscure soldier. With even greater enthusiasm he records the mutual chivalry and humanity of English and French officers throughout Marlborough's campaigns. But commonly his picture of warfare is sombre and contemptuous. Thus in discussing his first-hand materials for *Charles XII*, he writes: 'But if you examine the substance of the journal of M. Adlerfeld, what else do you find but: Monday April 3rd: So many thousand men slaughtered in such and such a place. Tuesday: Whole villages were reduced to ashes, women consumed by the flames with the children they held in their arms. Thursday: We annihilated with a thousand bombs the houses of a free and innocent town that failed to pay, money down, a thousand crowns to a foreign conqueror who passed its walls. Friday: Fifteen or sixteen hundred prisoners perished of hunger and cold. This is the theme, more or less, of four volumes.' With this talent of his for the faithful painting of the nude, he strides through the centuries, disrobing Glory. Who could forget his account of the last years of Louis XIV: victory abroad, famine at home: 'the people perished of hunger to the music of Te Deums.' He had often sojourned in Holland: from it he brought home a ghastly record of the barbarity of the French troops. If Louis had really vanquished the Dutch, 'who live by their commerce, or, if one may venture to say so, by their freedom, he would have won the deplorable glory of destroying the finest and most singular monument of human industry'. He has no illusions about the profits of victory. Sir Norman Angell might have written this passage: 'The victor nation never gains by despoiling the vanquished: it pays for everything: it suffers when its armies prosper as when they fail, and peace is almost as necessary to it, after the greatest victory, as when its enemies have taken its frontier posts.' The waste of war infuriates him: he says of the siege of Turin: 'Assuredly what was spent on all these preparations for destruction would have sufficed to found and render flourishing the most populous colony.' Here is his opinion of imperialism: 'For two centuries one of the consequences of the industry and fury of mankind has been that the desolation of our wars is no longer confined to Europe. We squander men and money in the effort to destroy one another in the farthest corners of Asia and America. The Indians, compelled by force and cunning to receive our factories, and the Americans whose Continent we have soaked in blood, regard us as the enemies of humanity, who run from the ends of the earth to slaughter them and thereafter to destroy ourselves.' There follows a deadly catalogue of devastations, one cold fact upon another. Finally, in an aside, he points to the remedy of arbitration. His comment on the Anglo-French quarrel over the boundaries of Canada is, that 'a similar dispute between two simple merchants would have been settled in a couple of hours by arbitrators'.

In spite of this reference to arbitration, Voltaire has little hope

that wars will cease. His sympathy with the Greeks even led him
to approve of Catherine's war of liberation. He thought the project of perpetual peace, drafted by the Abbé de Saint-Pierre and
popularized by Rousseau, a 'chimæra'. One sound objection he
raises—that it would not banish war, if Turkey and China were
excluded. For the rest he is content to say that man is a carni-
vorous animal and therefore will always fight. Was this a joke to
save the trouble of serious thinking? One is not sure, for the same
suggestion recurs in *The Princess of Babylon*, which one might
take to be a parable designed to inculcate vegetarianism. In several
scattered passages, indeed, he expresses a helpless horror at the
necessity of killing animals for food. There are two angry references in his writings to vivisection, and the Cartesian doctrine that
animals are automata always drove him into an intellectual rage.

The chief of the values that Voltaire held up to mankind was
humanity. To it and to liberty the force and passion of his genius
were dedicated. Cruelty he hated with an equal fury in detail and in
the mass, and he will turn with impartial rage on anyone, inquisitor
or king, soldier or statesman, who commits it. The sight of it, the
thought of it, roused him to the exercise of his most formidable
powers. If one were to collect from all his writings the passages that
stand out pre-eminent for their literary skill and wit, it is probable
that the greater number of them would prove to be protests against
cruelty. These verbal reprisals against brutality, especially when
they were directed against the idols of French tradition, must
have made a deep impact on the mind of his generation and the
next. Who could forget his account of the devastation of the Pala-
tinate, and his picture of Louis XIV, 'signing, amid his pleasures in
the depths of his palace of Versailles, the destruction of a whole
country'? Not the least effective touch in it is the cry: 'If he could
but have seen it, he would have put out the flames with his own
hands.' So from the raw material of history did Voltaire shape the
liberal tradition, a humane, a positive, a cosmopolitan attitude. It
won political liberty; it avoided economic equality; it has not
chained up war, and the workers, while still suitably poor, are very
often wretched.

V

THE MATCH WITH FREDERICK

Voltaire's decision to settle in Prussia made a clean breach with the French Court. Louis XV dismissed him from his post as Historiographer about the moment when the greatest work of history that Europe had seen, since the age of Tacitus, was ready for the press. Paris he was not to see again till this King was dead. This exile of twenty-eight years was a gain to literature, for had Voltaire remained in the capital he would have wasted on Fréron powers that belonged to mankind. The conservative part of the city rejoiced at his departure, and hawkers were selling in the streets for six sous engravings of 'Voltaire, the famous Prussian', wearing a bearskin to keep out the cold. In fact, the new climate suited him. He had seen to it that he should not lose by his removal, and Frederick called him his Danae, whom he had won in a shower of gold. He had the rank of Chamberlain, the cross of the Order of Merit, a pension of 29,000 francs, with 4,000 francs for his niece, the widowed Madame Denis, daughter of his sister Margaret, who kept his house in Paris. Potsdam, crowded with 150,000 victorious troops, made no very elegant background, but his reception at Sans-Souci dazzled him. Once more there were festivals: again his plays were acted by princes: he had never enjoyed such admiration in his life. He wrote that his tastes were in perfect agreement with Frederick's. His only duty was to give that monarch an hour's lesson daily in the elegancies of the French language, and to polish his poems for him. He heard all day his own language spoken round him, and indeed Frederick had only the most limited knowledge of German. He could give in it commands to his troops, but could not understand the simplest poem in his native language. Convenient as this denationalized culture may have been for a French guest, it meant that Voltaire, though his stay in Germany lasted longer than his stay in England, never penetrated its homely native life, and never learned its language. The poem on which the King was engaged was apparently an effort in the mock-heroic vein, as shocking as *The Maid*, and equally risky, for it dealt with contemporary events and reigning monarchs in a style offensive to the decencies. This lesson over, Voltaire was free to spend the day as he pleased. He avoided the royal dinner-table, at which there were too many princes and generals for his taste. He reserved his conversational virtuosity for the more congenial company that met every evening for a 'philosophic' supper in the King's private room. At these gatherings he sparkled, and enjoyed debating with his royal pupil every question that a daring and versatile mind could raise. Here there were no reticences and no fears. This Trajan was never at a loss for an answer.

It was a singular society, in which Voltaire found himself driven for the first time in his life to defend his sober and moderate opinions. For he was a deist among atheists. Intoxicated by his sudden freedom from a savage yoke, Frederick, after his father's death, gathered an astonishing round table of adventurers and exiles. 'His Humanity' sat unbuttoned in this company, but observed it shrewdly and was not overcome by respect. It was his feline way to caress with one paw and scratch with the other. To d'Argens, one of the members of this circle, he gave a house, but had it decorated with mural paintings representing the less edifying escapades in that adventurer's career. On Voltaire, he afterwards repeated this inhospitable joke; returning after an absence, he found the walls of his room decorated with apes, squirrels and peacocks. This king was not the first gentleman of Europe. Of Voltaire, at an early stage of his sojourn, he formed no very flattering opinion. 'I want to learn his French,' he wrote. 'What are his morals to me?'

If to live with this prince was good fortune, Voltaire, as usual, threw it away. Looking about, as his habit was, for a promising speculation, he heard of the notes of the Saxon Steuer-Bank. These issues of an exuberant printing-press were quoted in Dresden at a third of their face value. But in the recent treaty of peace, Frederick had required the King of Saxony to buy back at par such notes, to an unspecified total, as any Prussian subject might present. Shrewd persons in Berlin saw their opportunity, and Voltaire felt no scruples. He sent a certain Hirsch to Dresden on his behalf to buy these depreciated notes. Hardly had the Jewish banker reached Saxony, when Voltaire, who did not trust him, cancelled his order to buy. To cover up the transaction, and perhaps to compensate him for his trouble, Voltaire bought from Hirsch on his return some diamonds, which that financier overvalued. Though the amount of his loss was not heavy, the angry poet had the folly to go to law. The case went, on the whole, in his favour, but still the scandal stank. Frederick, ablaze with anger and contempt, refused to see him till his suit was settled, and then wrote him a stinging letter in which he admonished him to live like a philosopher. The supper-parties were resumed, and the spell of Voltaire's charm fell on the King again. But the gossips, as was natural, were busy. La Mettrie carried to Voltaire a saying of the King's: 'I shall have a use for him for a year at most: one squeezes the orange and throws away the skin.' Maupertuis, the French President of Frederick's Academy, whose nearer acquaintance we must now make, carried to the King an impatient remark of Voltaire's: 'Will he never tire of sending me his dirty linen to wash?'—by which he meant those exercises in French verse.

Maupertuis ranks among the more original personalities of this century. He came, as did also La Mettrie, from St. Malo, the adventurous citadel of the French privateers. A soldier in his youth, he studied mathematics and astronomy to such purpose that he won a seat in the Academy of Sciences. He visited England in 1728, became like Voltaire an ardent Newtonian, and was honoured by entry into the Royal Society. On his return to Paris he led the younger generation in a hot war of ridicule against the Cartesians. The controversy turned chiefly on the Newtonian theory of the flattened poles. To demonstrate it, Maupertuis led an expedition to Lapland to measure a degree of the meridian. It was for those days an unparalleled exploit, and Maupertuis returned to Paris, Newton's thesis demonstrated, with a legendary halo of glory about him. He was not a modest victor, and celebrated his triumph by writing a merciless satire on his opponents. He seemed to think, as Voltaire afterwards said, that he had himself flattened the poles, much as Atlas sustained the Heavens. Frederick now called him to Berlin;

he relished the wit and vivacity of Maupertuis, and made him President, with quasi-dictatorial powers, of his Academy. To his colleagues, in an address of monumental pomposity, he now communicated a discovery which he took to be epoch-making—a theory of the economy of Nature in physical causation. Of this theory the Swiss mathematician König wrote a courteous and even flattering criticism, in which he argued that within the narrow limits in which it is true, it had been anticipated by Leibnitz. He backed this statement by quotations from a letter in an unpublished series, of which a copy lay in the royal library of the Hague, of which he had charge. Unfortunately the originals of these letters were lost, which is not surprising, since the scholar to whom they were addressed had been executed. Maupertuis, in whom success had developed an intolerable arrogance, determined to destroy his critic. He caused a search to be made for the missing letters, though no competent student of Leibnitz has ever doubted the authenticity of the copies. When nothing could be found, he accused Professor König of forgery. Without giving that scientist an opportunity to appear in his own defence, he induced his docile Academy to censure and expel him. One may doubt whether in the history of science a man of Maupertuis' distinction has ever behaved towards an upright and capable colleague with such outrageous injustice.

This affair interested Voltaire, as it interested all Europe. Both men were his friends. Maupertuis had helped him with his letters on England, had been a visitor at Cirey, and a friend of Madame du Châtelet. König had been her teacher in mathematics, and in that capacity had spent two years at Cirey in close intimacy with both its inmates. It is probable that the tension of the morally unhealthy society of Sans-Souci had already weakened the friendship Voltaire felt for Maupertuis. But in the light of his whole career, when we ask what led him to support König, there is no need to look for hidden motives. A gross injustice had been done to a friend. It was Voltaire's habit in such cases to use all the resources of his genius to defend a stranger.

The dispute opened quietly. Voltaire wrote for publication a brief unsigned letter 'to an Academician of Paris', which simply marshalled the facts. No comment was needed. To this came in answer a long, ineffective, rhetorical letter, which handled Voltaire harshly. In place of a signature it bore on its title-page a crown, a sceptre and the Prussian eagle. At last Voltaire had an adversary worthy of his rapier, a philosopher-king. With this stimulus to his wit, he produced a masterpiece of light but deadly satire that has no equal in its kind. As one reads the outmoded types on the yellow pages, it seems as vivacious as on the day it was smuggled round a continent that rocked with laughter. For sustained fun, that rises in a continuous crescendo to a climax of rollicking hilarity, it has only one equal in literature, and that is De Quincey's *Essay on Murder*. It happened that Maupertuis had just published a rambling volume of speculations on cosmology, packed with some of the crudest absurdities that ever came from a learned pen. Voltaire saw his chance of making this autocrat of science ridiculous, and he invented an amusing fiction to achieve his purpose. Dr. Akakia, physician to the Pope, lays this work before the Inquisition. The Holy Office proceeds to quote some of the more startling of Maupertuis' heresies—his plan for prolonging life for several hundred years by stopping up the pores, his design to discover the nature of the soul by dissecting the twelve-foot giants of Australia, his scheme for digging a hole to the centre of the earth. One might have thought that the most inventive wit could add nothing to the fun of the quotations themselves, but Voltaire achieves it again and again, at the expense both of the Inquisition and of Maupertuis, in a solemn refutation of these errors. A treaty of peace is drawn up with König to prevent the further effusion of ink; Maupertuis promises to abandon digging and confine himself to the surface of things; he agrees to respect the equality of men of letters, by which he will gain; he recognizes that the test to which he subjected König would equally condemn the Holy Scriptures as forgeries. Finally, in a postscript, an actual letter from Maupertuis is quoted, in which he had threatened to give the good Dr. Akakia (Voltaire) a thrashing, and penalties of a delicate absurdity are imposed 'on the aforesaid philosopher and assassin'.

Frederick is not mentioned in this little pleasantry, but for Voltaire the cream of his joke doubtless was that he made use of a general licence to print, which the King in an expansive moment had given him, to have his pamphlet issued from the Royal Press. Part of the edition was seized in Berlin, but it was published simultaneously in Leipzig, and in Paris six thousand copies were sold in one day. On Christmas Eve, 1752, the executioner solemnly burned *The Diatribe of Dr. Akakia* at a cross-roads in Berlin, and Frederick consoled Maupertuis by sending him the ashes.

Voltaire anticipated no further enjoyment from the society of kings. 'Since I have not in this world 150,000 mustachios at my service,' he wrote to his niece, 'I do not pretend to make war. My only thought is how to desert decently . . . and forget this dream of three years. I see clearly that the orange has been squeezed: it is time to think of saving the skin.' He sent back to the King, with some pretty verses, his Chamberlain's key and the cross of his Order. Frederick seems to have been touched for a moment, for he restored to Voltaire these tokens of his esteem, and invited the poet to stay at Potsdam. He went, but only to take his leave. Pleading ill-health, he declared that only the waters of Plombières could save his life. Frederick's farewell was bluntly discourteous.

Voltaire was in no hurry to reach the waters of life, for he dawdled lengthily on his way. At Frankfurt, a free city, in which the King of Prussia had no jurisdiction, Voltaire, contrary to all the rules of international law, was arrested by his agents, and held in custody till he should deliver up his key, his cross and a volume of Frederick's poems. This seems to have been a privately printed copy of the mock-heroic indiscretion, which the royal pupil had given to his master. It was, unfortunately, in the heavy baggage that followed the traveller. His papers were searched and he was kept a close prisoner till it should arrive. When at last it came, Voltaire, having duly delivered it, made an attempt to drive off, only to be re-arrested at the city gates, and consigned under an armed guard to stricter and less honourable custody. This, Madame Denis, who meanwhile had joined her uncle, had to share, with much alarm on her part and much wrath on his. After a detention of six weeks, His Humanity at last sent orders for the poet's release. So ended Voltaire's stay in Prussia. He saw no more of Ferderick, but the oddest part of this story is that this monarch retained for the guest who had dared to answer him an admiration that prompted him in after years to renew their correspondence. Five years after these happenings, in the hour of Frederick's supreme disaster, Voltaire wrote to him to dissuade him from suicide and offered him a refuge on his own estate. In balancing their records, one reflects that while any man of letters would give a year of his life to have written Dr. Akakia's *Diatribe*, few kings would willingly shoulder responsibility for the brutal incident of Frankfurt.

For two years after this adventure Voltaire led a wandering life, still cherishing the vain hope that the road to Paris would be opened. He spent some time in Maintz and in Strasburg, and went to Colmar to see his *Annuals of the Empire* through the press. He read in the monastic library of Senones, and did at last drink the waters of Plombières. Passing through Lyons, he was amazed by the ovations he received in the theatre and at the academy of this town. Already the people were his partisans. Passing through Geneva, he was struck by the beauty of its situation, lingered, and finally in February, 1755, bought a villa by the lake which he named 'Les Délices, ('The Delight'). Its pastors felt some apprehension as he settled among them, but on the whole the city was flattered. At last he had a home, and earth to cultivate. In the freedom of this Republic he found the nearest substitute for peace and security that his restless spirit was capable of enjoying.

VI

'CANDIDE'

The earthquake that engulfed Lisbon in 1755 ranks among the decisive events of the eighteenth century. The destruction of the Cities of the Plain, four thousand years earlier, had set for the civilizations of the Eastern Mediterranean a similar problem. Orthodoxy in that age had found for it a simple and comforting solution: these cities had offended the police of the Universe by their abnormal wickedness. The eighteenth century was just struggling out of this naïve anthropocentric view. To call it the Age of Enlightenment, as historians commonly do, is to flatter it grossly. It was an age of rabid and cruel supersision. It still burned witches; kings still 'touched' for scrofula. An official astrologer, called to the royal bed-chamber, took the horoscope of Louis XIV as he came into this world; he quitted it wearing round his neck the bones of some departed saint that he might absorb their virtue, much as brown men will do to this day in the South Sea Islands. In Lisbon itself, the Holy Inquisition promptly appeased the wrath of Providence by burning a few Jews and heretics at the stake, whereupon a second shock shattered what was left of that city. None the less, on the fringes of all this official superstition, the Royal Societies and the Academies were busy, and with the Bronze Age view of life there co-existed a reluctant but fairly general belief that nature is governed by physical causation. On this first mechanistic glimpse of an orderly universe Leibnitz had built his celebrated system of optimism. Pope, with the help of Bolingbroke and Shaftesbury, popularized it in neat and pleasant verses, which soon appeared in an excellent French translation. It became the fashion in this complacent society to believe that all is for the best in the best of all possible worlds. Evil, to be sure, there is, but particular misfortunes viewed from a suitable distance are seen to compose the general good: many shadows are necessary in the scheme of any elaborate picture.

The enlightened man of fashion may not have grasped the lofty metaphysical pedantry from which Leibnitz deduced this comfortable doctrine, but it served the normal purpose of all correct philosophy. It reconciled him with things as they are, among them the shadowy miseries of the many and the substantial privileges of the few.

Voltaire in his early manhood was dazzled by this doctrine, and for a time Madame du Châtelet swallowed the Leibnitzian system whole. He had his doubts, as Zadig's eloquent 'But—' suggests. Some years passed, however, before he saw his way clearly through a rather elementary confusion. His final criticism, as witty and penetrating as need be, is to be found in his *Philosophic Dictionary* (Bien, tout est). Assuredly there is order everywhere. The agonies with which a stone in the bladder destroys a valuable life are a perfect illustration of physical causation and system. 'All is for the best' is true only in the sense that everything is subject to immutable laws. The doctrine is hardly consoling, and in addition it saps the Christian religion, since it deposes man from his seat as the centre of a creation designed for his good.

The event at Lisbon gave Voltaire the perfect text for a lay sermon on this theme. He set to work in creative excitement and produced in a few weeks his long poem on the earthquake. It is one of his best efforts in the style of this century, neatly phrased, closely reasoned, somewhat pedestrian in its orderly march, yet contriving to express sincerely and with a certain frank simplicity his distress, his perturbation at the unwelcome perception of a man's loneliness and impotence in a universe indifferent to his welfare. It ends with a confession of ignorance qualified by hope. The orthodox explanation is dismissed in a contemptuous line. Lisbon was no wickeder than other cities: 'Lisbon is ruined and we dance in Paris.' Leibnitz fares no better. Others, to be sure, may profit by my misfortunes, even by the death that ends my misery: 'A fine consolation to be eaten by worms.' There follow some passages that seem to be a conscious retraction of the most superficial of Voltaire's early works. With the letters on England he had published some *Preliminary Remarks on the Thoughts of M. Pascal* (1728). They reflect his temperamental dislike of Jansenism and his lifelong failure to understand a mystic. His own Deism permitted of the respect that a junior lieutenant in a smart uniform may feel towards an elderly and magnificent colonel. But the self-abasement of a finite creature before the infinite—this was as much beyond him as was Pascal's tormented sense of the dualism of human nature, its mingled pettiness and grandeur. Voltaire was always of a perfectly definite size, and that was not inconsiderable. In these *Remarks* he belaboured 'the sublime misanthrope' for belittling our species and 'addressing eloquent insults to the human race'. He quoted one of Pascal's cries, the passage in which he looks around him, perceives that 'the universe is dumb, man without light, abandoned to his own devices, lost in his corner of the earth, and unable to say who put him there or why, or what will come of him after death'; whereupon Pascal wonders that on 'this desert island' man can escape despair. Voltaire's reply was that of a monumentally insensitive man of fashion: 'For my part, when I look at Paris or London, I see no reason to indulge in this despair of which M. Pascal speaks. I see a city that in no way resembles a desert isle. It is populous, wealthy, civilized, and in it men are as happy as human nature permits.'

The poem on Lisbon actually contains some echoes of Pascal, which must have been conscious. 'Nature is dumb, one questions her in vain.' The conclusion, which one may translate thus, is worth quoting, for it reveals a new Voltaire:

> Atoms tormented on this ball of clay,
> The sport of death, of hazard's strokes the prey,
> Yet thinking atoms, atoms whose clear eyes
> Guided by thought have measured out the skies,
> Into the infinite we fling our gaze
> Yet cannot see ourselves, nor count our days...
>
> Humbly I sigh, submissive I await
> Without a challenge the decrees of fate.
> More cheerfully, indeed, in bygone times
> I sang of pleasure in seductive rhymes.
> The times are changed and age has schooled my mind
> To share the common frailties of mankind.
> Groping in darkness for a guiding light
> No murmur shall escape me in the night.

A dying Caliph, sick upon his bed
Turned to the God he loved, in prayer, and said,
'My King, I bring thee with my gratitude
All that thou lackest in thy plenitude.
Sin, ignorance and suff'ring and regret.'
But why did he the best gift, hope, forget?

This poem, which appeared with another on *Natural Law*, a
rather bolder exposition of the tolerant, deist creed, was punctually
burned by order of the Parlement of Paris (1759). A more closely
reasoned refutation was furnished by Jean-Jacques Rousseau, of all
men. In a not over-friendly letter he remonstrated with 'this poor
man, overwhelmed, so to speak, with prosperity and glory, who
bitterly declaims against the wretchedness of this life'. One smiles at
this thrust, yet it was to the credit of this rich man that he did not
confuse his own good fortune with the common lot. Out of this
controversy sprang the one book of Voltaire's that is certainly
immortal, his tale, *Candide* (1758).

Twice Voltaire seemed to have won immortality. His tragedies
were, while he lived, the broad foundation of his fame. He had surpassed, it was thought, the Greeks, the rough English, the exuberant Spaniards, all his contemporaries, everyone, indeed, save
Corneille and Racine. In his later years and for a generation or two
after his death, what men read most eagerly were his histories and
the pocket *Philosophic Dictionary*. These formed the mind of liberal
Europe. The plays are dead. The graver prose works have ceased
to be the indispensable possession of everyone who reads. But
Candide lives on, and one may read it in any civilized tongue, in
rich editions illustrated by great artists, or in paper covers sold for a
few pence. The writer cherishes a cheap copy bought in a remote
little town in Turkey, that has passed in his recollection through
most of the vicissitudes known to Voltaire's hero; for it has seen a
massacre, a conflagration, a siege, a bombardment, and three successive conquests. He read it as he camped among burned villages,
and watched three epidemics in one winter decimate the population
that had survived the artillery and the flames. In those surroundings
there was much to be said for its argument, that this is not the best

of all possible worlds. It is probable that it will never go wholly out of date.

What shall one call it? A tale, a satire, a philosophical romance that describes the life of Everyman? It is all these things, but also it is the most perfect model of written prose, in the language that is of all European tongues the best adapted for this art. You will not lay it down, if once you take it up, and as the years crowd upon you, you will find that you can read it over and over again. It is like a quartette of Mozart's: so light it seems, so graceful, so easy, that one supposes that none of its beauties can escape an attentive ear at the first playing, yet every repetition is discovery. Is it a tale? Then the story is at once the simplest and the most fantastic that ever came from the pen of man. The characters are thin outlines of humanity. The moral is obtrusive. What is it, then, that hurries the reader along enthralled? Partly it is the play of wit. Partly it is the fun of watching this preposterous thesis of optimism poked and tossed and chased and mauled with the most perfect grace and good manners, much as a mother cat may tease a clumsy kitten. Partly it is the never-failing invention. Lest we should tire of the crude horrors of the wars of the Bulgarians and the Abars, the earthquake at Lisbon, the prim brutalities of the Inquisition and the adventures of a Pope's bastard among Moorish pirates, there comes the relief of Candide's sojourn in Eldorado, and thereafter the highly sophisticated corruptions of Paris. With what perfect stage management are we introduced to the eerie supper party of the six dethroned kings, 'who had come to pass the Carnival at Venice'. With what art is that refrain repeated, and how tactfully we decline from the tragedy of the Sultan, the Tsar, Charles Edward Stuart and the two Kings of Poland, to the farce of Theodore of Corsica. The end of the whole story might seem idyllic, for in the tranquil garden by the Bosphorus, Candide, after all his harrowing adventures, has at last domesticated and even married the lady of his youthful passion, Mlle Cunégonde. This world, if not the best, wags passably well. But there are shadows. The lady has grown ugly and peevish, and as we talk in the miniature Eden, two viziers and the mufti have just been strangled and several of their friends impaled.

The tale, we said, is fantastic. It is so, however, only by accumulating an incredible number of extreme misfortunes on a single head. Candide is the Pilgrim of this Progress, the Everyman of this Mystery. He suffers nothing that is not the common lot. Voltaire is playing an absorbing game with us. The rules of it are strict enough. The king of his chessmen bears a charmed life—neither beatings, tempests, an earthquake, an *auto-da-fé*, a duel, nor even the attentions of French physicians can end it: Candide must stay on the board. But it is understood that no single incident in all the heaped-up horrors, all the multiplied coincidences, shall be in itself incredible, or even improbable. We watch Voltaire, but we never catch him out. Many of these incidents are actually historical—the earthquake, the subsequent doings of the Inquisition, the war against the Jesuit colony of Paraguay, the execution of Admiral Byng. The great actress who played Queens of England in Paris was really buried in a ditch. The six dethroned kings were all contemporaries. Do you doubt that a well-born young man could be kidnapped for a foreign army in Westphalia, and all but skinned alive when he tried to desert? Voltaire met this person, a French chevalier, lacking his nose and ears, as he trundled a wheelbarrow in the royal garden at Potsdam. King Frederick William's press-gang snatched him with many another, but he was the only one whom Voltaire could rescue by writing a set of verses. What else is improbable? Not the galleys rowed by slaves and convicts. Voltaire himself got some of them released. Do you doubt that a philosopher may catch the disease that Columbus brought to Europe? Maupertuis had that misfortune. As for Paquette, she endured only what all young women who drift into her profession must expect. Negro slavery was pretty much as Voltaire describes it at Surinam; indeed, he relates elsewhere this instance of it as a fact. Unwilling monks must often have suffered the distress that demoralized Brother Giroflée. Within the rules of the game, this is a veracious chronicle.

The reader need have no fear of wallowing in all these horrors. There is not a tear among them. Dr. Pangloss, who was hanged and thereafter dissected, is too well-mannered to exact this tribute. There are two ways of confronting cruelty and wrong. The more usual attitude, in countries of Anglo-Saxon speech, is to spend oneself in pity for the victim. This is productive of much disinterested distress and of guineas for Mansion House funds. The cruelty, none the less, persists. Pity, when all is said, is the last insult. It injures him who gives and him who takes. It was not Voltaire's way, though in real life it is recorded of him several times that he wept. His tears were not for paper. His answer to cruelty and wrong was militancy, reckless and merciless. Since, as he used to say, he had not 'a hundred thousand mustachios at his command', his warfare was necessarily intellectual. He used that wit which is the Sword of the Spirit, piercing every joint of the Breastplate of Self-Righteousness. His thrusts, given a little time, were frequently mortal. A fair number of the wrongs and cruelties he assailed fell to his strokes. It is a common objection to this use of the intellect, that it is negative. This is singular logic. Every negation implies an affirmation. While Voltaire attacks, you may hear his credo chanted to the rhythm of his blows. When he renders cruelty hateful and injustice contemptible, he that has ears to hear will catch above the battle his hymn to brotherly love.

One asks how the thing is done. Wit so various and supple obeys no formula. But one secret of his power we can detect. He had the art of stripping human actions and relations of the trappings of abstract words in which they commonly go draped. He will not say that heretics were executed in an *auto-da-fé*. He tells us plainly that they were roasted over a slow fire. Listen to his account of the judicial murder of Admiral Byng, as Candide saw it. 'Conversing in this way, they landed at Plymouth. A multitude of people covered the shore, and stared attentively at a rather burly man who was kneeling, his eyes bandaged, on the deck of one of the warships. Four soldiers, posted in front of this man fired, each of them, three bullets into his skull in the most peaceful way in the world, and the whole assemblage went home extremely satisfied.' This is perfectly concrete, treasonably concrete. It compels us to see exactly what was done with a directness of vision of which few persons in that multitude can have been capable. The case is then analysed. Candide learns that Byng was shot 'because he did not cause enough men to be killed: he gave battle to a French admiral, and the verdict was that he was not near enough to him'. 'But,' said Candide, 'the French admiral was just as far from the English admiral, as the Englishman was from the Frenchman.' And then comes one of those swift, disconcerting thrusts to which there is no parry known. 'In this country, it is well from time to time to kill an admiral to encourage the others.' One might illustrate this method indefinitely: first see, with perfect definition, in the round, the cruelty in question: then thrust with the utmost economy of movement. One may choose at random another instance from *Candide*. That traveller saw at Surinam a nigger, clad only in a pair of drawers, who lacked the left leg and the right hand, waiting for his master, M. Vanderdendur, the famous merchant. 'Did he use you thus?' 'Yes, sir,' said the negro, 'it is the custom. They give us a pair of drawers, as our only clothing, twice a year. When we work at the sugarmills, if the machinery catches a finger, they cut off a hand: when we try to escape, they cut off a leg: both things happened to me.' Then comes the thrust. 'That is the price at which you eat sugar in Europe.'

But there is more in this tale than effective satire. Under all the bitter gaiety, there runs a parable of man's life on this earth, that is not without tenderness and kindly wisdom. This youth of excellent parts but great simplicity is the immortal idealist whose pilgrimage through life others also have traced. He is a juvenile Quixote; he is a less sedentary Faust. Though born in Westphalia, his mind had a positive quality that is wholly French. He fought no windmills; he had no truck with phantoms. He knew precisely what he wanted, to embrace Mlle Cunégonde, whom he once had kissed behind a screen. Yet for the ideal, in this pleasing corporeal form, did he not undertake a quest through battles and tempests across two continents and against the leagued powers of kings and priests, that might have done honour to any Knight of the Holy Grail? Him also 'the eternal womanly' drew onwards. He travelled, indeed, with French eyes through an eighteenth-century world. Here were no Brocken spectres, no Helen, no homunculus, nothing at all of that thronged menagerie of symbols that peoples infinity for the Teutonic imagination. But was there not in his insatiable search, told to be sure in excellent French prose, something of that craving, for the ideal that ever eludes us, which men of other races and other centuries have described in language of a conscious exaltation? Candide was what Oswald Spengler calls a Faustian man: he craved, if not infinity, yet in no finite way, He met, as the idealist in this world-wide myth always meets, with disillusion. His Cunégonde, when he attained her, was ugly and old. The quest in the end was not worth achieving. And yet, not unlike the aged Faust, in creative work he found happiness. The parable of human life ends commonly in this way, though few have told its moral with the satisfying concrete-ness of this French romance. There is at its edifying close none of that choir of angels dropping roses that the German Goethe pro-vided. But Voltaire assures us that Mlle Cunégonde became an excellent pastry-cook, and the whole society was passably happy, since they had learned to cultivate their garden.

Candide ranks first among the many tales that Voltaire tossed off in the intervals between the really serious business, as he con-ceived it, of writing his forgotten tragedies. Three of them are hardly inferior in wit and invention to his masterpiece, if inferior they be—*Zadig* (1748) which we have already described; *Micro-megas* (1752); and *L'Ingénu* (1767). Nothing that he ever wrote could lack vitality, and all his tales are worth reading, but the rest of them are slighter and less powerful than the four best. One may single out three of these. *Babouc; or, The Way of the World* (1746) was his first effort. It is a report written by a wise Scythian for the angel Ithuriel, who was doubtful whether he should destroy the wicked city of Persepolis. The social life of Paris is described, and though the conclusion is in the end favourable, there is scope enough for gentle satire. Unlike Jonah, who was distressed that Nineveh escaped destruction, Babouc was much relieved. 'But when one has spent three days in the belly of a whale, one is not so good-hu-moured, as when one has been to the opera and the comedy and supped in good company.' *The History of Scarmentado's Travels* (1747) bristles with wit, and is a brief summary view of the cruelty and intolerance prevalent on this earth, that reads like a first rapid sketch of the involuntary voyage of discovery that Candide after-wards undertook. *The Princess of Babylon* (1768) starts as the simp-lest of oriental fairytales, and then turns into yet another tour of exploration through Europe. The surprising part of it is that while Paris and Spain are found to be as corrupt and ill-governed as ever, the North, from Russia to England, reveals the triumph of philosophy. The Empress Catherine and the kings who were Voltaire's pupils enjoy their master's smile.

Micromegas stands out from the rest as one of the most brilliant philosophical romances ever written. It is an account of the visit to our earth of a gigantic inhabitant of Sirius and a dwarf from Saturn. The germ of this tale came from *Gulliver's Travels*, but Voltaire's mood in this piece is incomparably more urbane and genial than Swift's. He pokes some gentle fun at Fontenelle who sat for the portrait of the scientists from Saturn, and in the course of their investigations the two celestial visitors pick up in their hands the microscopic ship in which Maupertuis and his companions were returning from Lapland: Dr. Akakia's victim is treated in this tale with friendly good-humour. The simplest of Voltaire's contemporary readers would voyage with him from planet to planet mightily entertained by the rollicking fun of the adventure. But any lingering vanity he may have cherished about the place of our earth in the universe and the importance of man in the scheme of creation would be completely dissipated. Somewhere between the discoveries of Copernicus and those of Newton, the anthropocentric view ought to have vanished from human thinking. In this tale Voltaire finally extinguishes it in laughter. With a tiny disciple of Locke who was on board this ship the two gigantic philosophers from the stars got on very well. 'But unluckily there was there a little animalcule in a square cap, who cut the speeches of the philosophic animalcules short; he said that he knew the whole secret; it was to be found in the *Summa* of Saint Thomas; he looked the two celestial beings up and down, and maintained that their persons, their worlds, their suns, their stars were all created solely for man. At this speech our two travellers gave way, one after the other, to that choking, inextinguishable laughter, which is, according to Homer, peculiar to the gods: their shoulders and stomachs came and went, and in these convulsions the ship that the Sirian held on his fingernail fell into the pocket of the Saturnian's breeches.'

L'Ingénu (Master Simple) is in a wholly different manner. It is a contemporary tale. Nothing fantastic, nothing even improbable happens in it. An untamed Huron from French Canada lands in

Brittany and makes the acquaintance of French civilization. At first, the fun of his stumblings, his bewilderments, his criticisms and his astonishing discoveries among this nation of strange morals and stranger beliefs is what one would expect from Voltaire. It is irresistibly amusing, while it plays happily enough over the surface of things. But on his way to Paris this most sympathetic of savages encounters in an inn some Huguenots who were being driven from their fatherland. The atmosphere, which had been so light and carefree in Brittany, grows sultry, and the wit, that only tickled in the early pages, now thrusts and stabs. Voltaire, in his own characteristic fashion, is in deadly earnest. Presently the Huron finds himself in the Bastille with a surprisingly likeable Jansenist, and Voltaire paints for us the corrupt world of courtiers, ministers and Jesuit confessors with a merciless, if polished bitterness. Towards the end his manner changes again. Mlle Saint-Ives, the Huron's Breton lady-love, journeys to Paris to rescue him, is seduced by a minister in her anxiety to buy his freedom, and dies of shame. Voltaire has slid into the vein of Richardson, though he is as brief and direct and salt as one could wish. For once he allows himself pathos, and succeeds. This tale is one of the most puzzling feats in literature. None of the characters, and least of all the lady, has the substance of corporeal human beings. They are all merely suggested in the thin outlines congenial to Voltaire's pencil. Though we know that these caricatures of the great Louis' confessors and ministers have a deadly resemblance to the originals, this world, as Voltaire paints it, is none the less fantastic, for wit has the effect of summer lightning upon a nocturnal landscape: it renders it unreal. And yet the end of this tale has power to move us. The waste and the pity of it distress us, and we rise from it amazed at the paradoxical magic of this artist, who heaps up every obstacle against himself and yet contrives to reach our emotions.

Voltaire set no store by his tales. Unconsciously and without effort he produced a series of masterpieces. It was a form of literature in which this age excelled, but Montesquieu came nowhere near him in wit, polish and grace. Swift, if he surpassed him in brutal power, has nothing of his charm. Sterne, compared with him, is a miniaturist, perfect in his little art. Taken as a whole, these tales present us with a lively picture of eighteenth-century Europe as a shrewd and virile observer of immense experience perceived it. It was, one gathers, very far from being a credit to Providence. It was not the best of all possible worlds. But this philosopher was no pessimist. This world had its redeeming features. There were Jesuits in it, insolent aristocrats and brutal war-lords at whom it was a pleasant exercise to tilt.

VII

HE CULTIVATES HIS GARDEN

One of the best of Voltaire's poems (*The author arriving on his estate*, 1755) records in eloquent and harmonious verse what he felt about Geneva. He sings the serenity of the lake, the flowers and vines upon its shores, the frowning beauty of its mountain rampart. He reminds himself of the history graven on these rocks, and then recalls Vergil and his Italian lakes. But on their banks he flattered a tyrant. There follows a fine hymn to Swiss liberty. Wordsworth's sonnet is nobler and terser than Voltaire's ode, but the longer poem is none the less moving and sincere. One feels in it the man expanding, as for the second time in his life, after an interval of a quarter of a century, he breathed free air. He prays that liberty and friendship may preside over his last days. In fact they brought him a renewal of his youth. These 'last days' ran on for three and twenty years, which were the happiest and most productive of his long life. Lake, mountains and republican liberty could not make of this turbulent spirit a patient or complacent man. He fights on with all his old unbending militancy, but there is more purpose and concentration in his warfare, and he fritters less of his time and energy on personal quarrels. He bends his great powers to a disinterested struggle for humanity.

A wholly new Voltaire emerges from contact with the earth. When Candide drew the final moral from his astonishing experience of life, that 'one should cultivate one's garden', he was using a pregnant metaphor. Doubtless 'one's garden', as Voltaire used the words, is a name for any field of positive, creative activity. It may include the cultivation of the arts: it certainly means building and even manufacture, any effort, in short, that has a direct social purpose, anything that betters the environment in which one's fellow-men must spend, under the shadows of terror, misfortune and wickedness, their brief and precarious years. But above all, it means, literally, the cultivation of the soil. In ploughed fields lies the main source of human wealth and well-being. This many-sided man succeeded at last in simplifying himself. The final revaluation of values, on which throughout his career he was engaged, was an exaltation, above all the artificial life of courts and cities, of the creative work of the husbandman. At the end of a long letter written in 1760, after some lively literary criticism devoted to Richardson and Rabelais, he suddenly broke off: 'But there are pleasures superior to all this sort of thing: to see the grass grow in the fields, and the abundant harvest ripen. That is man's true life: all the rest is vanity.' Virtue comes to mean something perfectly concrete—the draining of swamps, the building of roads and bridges, the planting of trees. Voltaire was almost angrily contemptuous of Rousseau's enthusiasm for the noble savage and life according to nature. He was not impressed, among these barren Swiss mountains, by the bounty and beneficence of nature: he had the farmer's passion to tame her and subjugate her. He would have laughed mercilessly at Tolstoy's enthusiasm for the godly peasant. The peasants whom he learned to know seemed to him only a little above the level of the beasts. In a poem dedicated to Henri IV he wrote:

> On these piled mountains, frozen by the gale,
> In hollow rocks and fearsome cañons pent,
> What are these beasts, thin, ugly, pale,
> Naked and hungry, 'neath misfortune bent?
> Yet they are men: and it is Nature's way
> Even on these in bounty to bestow,
> While with her hands she shapes their mortal clay
> And forms the instinct their rude movements show,
> All that she gave to Rome's victorious breed.

So far is he from idealizing these peasants, that his thoughts were constantly engaged with plans to raise them in the social scale.

There was a garden round his Genevan villa, and he began by cultivating it with enthusiasm. But he was not content for long with 'Les Délices'. It was exposed to the north wind in winter, and to escape it he migrated in the colder months to Lausanne. Another reason influenced him. Geneva was a free Republic, but it was governed by its conservative upper middle class and by its Calvinist pastors. In due course, Geneva burned *Candide* in its market-place (1759), and when Voltaire began, as his custom was, to give private performances of classical plays at 'Les Délices', the Presbytery addressed to him a stern remonstrance. Lausanne was less puritanical, and there he could indulge his passion for acting without interference. An even better opportunity soon presented itself. Two adjoining estates, Ferney and Tournay, in French territory but actually on the frontier, at the confines of Geneva itself and close to 'Les Délices', were for sale, and in 1755 he bought them. He now had a choice of asylums. If Louis XV were to issue a 'sealed letter' against him, he had only to step into Switzerland, while from Calvinist intolerance he could flee as readily to Catholic soil. His mischievous sense of humour enjoyed erecting a miniature theatre on his French esate, which was soon thronged by the citizens of Geneva, who could now enjoy this ungodly pleasure out of reach of a Presbytery which still sat as a tribunal of morals to judge the private life of every burgher.

Voltaire's chief reason, however, for acquiring Ferney, was the passion for the land that had seized him. The soil was barren: both estates had long been neglected, and both manor-houses were dilapidated. The few inhabitants were housed in hovels. At once, with a lavish use of his considerable fortune, he set to work to make of Ferney a model community. 'The true philosopher,' he wrote in a letter to a friend, 'is he who clears uncultivated ground, adds to the number of ploughs, and so to the number of inhabitants.' He repaired the roads and built new ones. He drained the marshes. He built cottages and a homestead, and enlarged the manor-house. He was determined that every man who lived on his land should have work, and should be well paid for it. He became one of the pioneers of scientific forestry, and after gathering from the few experts of this time the best advice he could get, he started planting trees for timber, fuel and fruit on a magnificent scale. He learned to supervise the work of a considerable farm not only with delight and enthusiasm, but with an intelligence rarely devoted in those days to agriculture. In a long description of his farm there are several sentences about his animals that reveal a gentleness at which no careful reader of Voltaire will feel surprise. There was a field, used apparently for experimental crops, which no one else might touch, and though it seems incredible, there is good authority for the statement that until extreme old age came upon him, he actually ploughed it himself.

Voltaire was lord of the manor, as well as farmer, and he took his duties seriously. He did not believe that labourers could be weaned from the Church. He pulled down the dilapidated chapel of Ferney and raised a graceful classical building in its place, which bore the inscription: *Deo erexit Voltaire* (Voltaire built it for God). The deist would not dedicate his chapel to a saint, but when the clergy began to worry him about it, he silenced them by repeating the joke he had played over his play *Mahomed*. He asked for a relic from the Pope, and got it. Needless to say, he waged an intermittent guerrilla warfare with his bishop and the local clergy. He delivered his vassals from a despotic priest, whose brutality was, one trusts, exceptional, for he kept gangsters who would beat any parishioner who opposed or disobeyed him, to the peril of his life. He took a pleasure one can understand in counteracting the acquisitive habits of neighbouring monastic houses, and on one occasion, at some cost to himself, saved the ancestral fields of three orphans from the Jesuits. These were small things, however, and he knew that something much more fundamental was required before the peasantry could even begin to prosper. Like all the liberals of his day, he had always been the bitter critic of the whole system of taxation under the Monarchy. Now, at close quarters, he saw how it fleeced the peasants, who were, he insisted, the most productive part of the nation. He wrote at this time (1767) a popular tract, in the form of a tale with dialogues, *The Man with Forty Crowns*. It described the life of the average peasant who drew from his land an income of forty crowns a year, and paid away half of it under the mad species of single tax that prevailed at this period. It pointed to the immunity from taxation of the merchants and speculators who throve by handling this peasant's grain. From this it passed to the congenial theme of the idle monastic orders. It is, with all its lightness of form, a powerful exposure of the licensed robbery of the working peasant, or at least of such aspects of it as this liberal

D

century chose to notice. It is, in its way, one of the most effective
things that ever came from Voltaire's pen. It was meant for the
plain man and it reached him. Through the next twenty years this
tale did its work quietly, and one can trace its influence in the
'cahiers' of 1789. But Voltaire was not working for a revolution;
he was the typical liberal reformer, who never disdained to toil for
small improvements, even local improvements, if he could get
them here and now. Turgot's brief spell of power at the Ministry of
Finance filled him with high hopes, and he used his credit with his
fellow 'philosopher' to obtain the remission, or rather the com-
mutation on easy terms, of the worst of the taxes, the 'ferme' (i.e.
farmed tax), under which his impoverished Alpine county of Gex
was groaning. His reception, when he drove with a mounted
escort of his tenants, to the meeting of the Estates of Gex, to get this
achievement ratified, was one of the high moments of his career. In
another attempt of the kind he failed, but to fail in an elementary
reform of humanity, when the effort was made by a man of genius
in vain, was to hasten on the Revolution. Nominally serfdom had
been abolished in France in the thirteenth century; actually it survived in some regions as long as the Monarchy itself. One of these
was Franche-Comté, at Voltaire's door. The feudal overlords were
the monks of Saint-Claude, who seem to have administered their
odious rights with harsh severity. Their serfs appealed to Voltaire,
and with his usual energy he did his utmost for them. He wrote
with all his biting wit on this tempting subject, but he also helped
them to carry their case to the courts and to the Ministry. By the
feudal rule of 'mortmain', the whole property of every inhabitant,
unless his children had lived all their lives without a break under
their father's roof, fell at his death to the monks. His widow and
children, without a roof, furniture, money or even clothes, were reduced to beggary. Voltaire achieved less than nothing: these feudal
rights of property were actually confirmed.

Two new connections claimed part of Voltaire's abounding
energy during the Genevan period. A philosopher-queen had
risen on his horizon. He had his doubts at first about Catherine II of
Russia: she had some crimes to her account that it was difficult to
forget. Voltaire was equal to that feat, however, and after an ex-

change of letters in which her flattery answered his gallantry, he formed a fantastically exaggerated idea of the scope and effect of her reforms. By the end of his life he believed that the whole north of Europe was won for 'philosophy'. His age and fame had made him the recognized leader of an international 'philosophic' party. His juniors journeyed to Geneva or Ferney for advice, and he kept contact with them all in an active correspondence, in which he spurred them on to greater zeal, and often gave sagacious counsel on the tactical conduct of their common war against 'superstition'. D'Alembert was a guest at 'Les Dèlices', and with Voltaire he discussed his great project, the 'Encyclopædia'. It was conceived not merely as a worthy and accurate summary of all the knowledge that the century of enlightenment had won, above all in the field of physical science and technology. It was also the manifesto of the philosophic party, which should carry on the war against superstition, and advocate the political programme of the liberals over its whole range—the reform of legal and fiscal abuses, the abolition of class privileges, the adoption of freedom of conscience and trade (for Voltaire now begins to link these two, with no sense of incongruity). From the start the patriarch gave to D'Alembert and Diderot, the real hero of this great constructive adventure, his warm encouragement. He wrote many articles for them, and would turn his hand to any task, however humble, content, as he put it, to play the apprentice in their workshop. He shared their regret at the compromises to which they were sometimes driven, and stood by them stoutly, when the inevitable vexations of suppression and condemnation delayed but never stopped their work.

On his return to Paris D'Alembert wrote for the 'Encyclopædia' the famous article on Geneva. It was a friendly eulogy of the city, which praised its enlightenment, envied its liberty, and attributed to its pastors a liberal faith which even the younger of them dared not avow. The statement that they were virtually Unitarians, who had rejected supernatural religion, infuriated the Protestant clergy and was solemnly repudiated. A gentle hint that the Genevan horror of stage plays was hardly worthy of the high culture of the city led to a controversy which left its mark on the history of literature. Voltaire was thought to have inspired this article, and when J.-J.

Rousseau replied to it in his celebrated letter on 'Spectacles' (1758),
he made a direct attack on the poet, as a foreigner who was cor-
rupting with his private theatre the simple republican morals of his
native city. This was the more odd because the French classical
theatre, from Corneille to Voltaire, was a school of the most elevated and self-conscious morality. What induced Rousseau, who
was himself a passionate lover of the theatre and the author of some
plays and operas, to write this masterpiece of paradox, is one of the
psychological puzzles that teem in his career. He was himself a
'philosopher' and a valued contributor to the Encyclopædia, but he
had already conceived a morbid suspicion of Voltaire, that soon
deepened into one of his characteristic manias of persecution. Their
early intercourse had been slight but perfectly friendly. But Voltaire
extravert, classic and rationalist, was not made to admire this intro-
verted, emotional romantic. He wrote a pleasant, chaffing letter
about Rousseau's essay on the 'Inequality among Men': with *Émile*
he was bored, though he gave to the 'Savoyard Vicar' the most
generous praise. When, however, the news reached Voltaire, that a
warrant was out in Paris for Rousseau's arrest, he wept (the scene
is described by a visitor) and declared with generous vehemence,
'Let him come here and I'll treat him like a son.' Not knowing where
to find the fugitive, he sent out seven copies of a letter inviting him
to settle as his guest in a cottage on the Ferney estate. There is
evidence that one of these letters, at least, reached its destination.
Soon afterwards Rousseau repaid this kindly action with a meanness that Voltaire never forgave. In one of his combative 'Letters
from the Mountain', addressed to Geneva, he referred pointedly to
The Sermon of the Fifty as a work of Voltaire's. This was the
boldest attack on Christianity that the old Deist had yet risked, and
it had come from the press without his name—a usual precaution in
this century. It was circulating in Geneva in great numbers, scattered by zealous but unknown hands in many ingenious ways, to
the rage and horror of the authorities. The artisan watchmakers,
whose champion in their battle for political rights Voltaire was,
seem to have been his agents in this subterranean propaganda. To
identify this shocking pamphlet as his work was to denounce him
to the Magnificent Council, which was quite capable of imprisoning

the author of books it had already burned. Voltaire, who was now helping the popular side, 'the natives', in their civil strife against the 'citizens'—plutocrats 'who wanted liberty', as he put it, 'only for themselves'—had tried to mediate to no purpose. When that effort failed, he wrote a rather poor mock-heroic poem, *The War of Geneva*, in which he laughed at the puritan intolerance of the city, amused himself with the controversy over the theatre, and introduced a satire on Rousseau, unworthy either of his wit or his good taste. He was, doubtless, entitled to his revenge, but that a sane and healthy mental athlete should attack a mental invalid, and thereby aggravate his disease, was not the act of a good man. One regrets his epigrams on Rousseau even when they are just. But this suffering 'dog' had in fact a habit of 'biting the hand that caressed him'. Rousseau treated Diderot and David Hume, both of them his generous friends, with the same mad hostility. One likes to put it on record that in 1772 Rousseau contributed his subscription to Pigalle's statue of Voltaire, as also did Frederick the Great. When on a later occasion he was invited to write an attack on Voltaire, he refused. 'No doubt,' he wrote, 'he is a malevolent man, as I know to my cost, but he has said and done so many good things, that we must draw a veil over his eccentricities.'

The civil strife in Geneva was now to people Ferney. Voltaire welcomed the many refugees and built houses for them. By 1767 he had on his land a numerous colony, which included a surgeon, an apothecary, several merchants and many artisans. His first scheme to find work for this growing population was to develop a silk industry. He had planted mulberry groves, and now he turned his theatre into a factory. Every step in the process, from the rearing of the silkworms to the weaving of the stockings, was done on his estate, under his supervision. He was proud of his triumph over a difficult climate, for snow lay for seven months of the year at Ferney, and he boasted that his silk was better than that of Provence or Italy. He also manufactured silk cloth, and organized a home industry for the women, who made a species of Brussels lace. Most of his refugees, however, were watchmakers, and of these he soon had about a hundred, with their families. He housed them all, and lent them capital to carry on their skilled trade. Better still, he organized their

market for them, and mobilized all his friends among the great to sell
their watches. His influence did not avail to open the gates of Paris
to himself, but it served to set all the embassies of France touting for
the products of his watchmakers. He conscripted a Cardinal to
find him a reliable agent in Rome. All his admirers among the kings
of Europe had to buy, and Catherine of Russia, now at war with
Turkey, was a lavish purchaser. 'May they bring many a bad quarter
of an hour to Mustapha,' he wrote, as he dispatched her case of
watches. Simultaneously he sold equally good watches to the said
Mustapha, and so anticipated the modern dealers in armaments who
supply both sides in wartime—but his was an innocent munition.
His letters and circulars are marvels of literary salesmanship, and as
one reads their descriptions of the miracles of taste and ingenuity
that Ferney could produce, at one third less than the usual price,
one finds oneself regretting that one was born into this world too
late to buy these watches.

So life ran on at Ferney. Voltaire would still write a tale, or polish
a tragedy by way of distraction, but the main stream of his still
abounding energies was divided between two preoccupations, care
for his colony and the unending war on superstition. An incessant
trickle of visitors flowed through Ferney—'philosophers' of all
nations, French actors and actresses, young literary men like La
Harpe, and English tourists, Boswell among them. At times they
were an affliction, and he had difficulty in dodging the attentions of
the curious. To an Englishman, on one occasion, he excused himself on the ground that he was ill. That failed. 'Tell him I'm dying,'
said Voltaire, but the fellow still insisted. 'Tell him I'm dead,' was
the next message, but the man still wished to pay his last respects.
'Then tell him that the devil has carried me off,' was Voltaire's
parting shot.

In these last years he had his little group of intimates about him.
His niece, Mme Denis, a fat, lively, bustling little woman, who
acted and wrote verses, amused him and adored him. He petted her,
teased her, and always ended by doing her bidding. For a time there
was Corneille's grand-niece, whom he rescued from poverty and
adopted, to do honour to his master in tragedy. She seems to have
been a good but commonplace young woman, and she married

young. For thirteen years Voltaire gave a refuge at Ferney to a fugitive Jesuit, Father Adam. He was not, as Voltaire put it, 'the first of mankind', but he played chess well, and this philosopher liked to be impartial in succouring the victims of sectarian strife. His favourite among the inmates of his house was a young girl whom he had rescued from a convent and adopted. Mlle de Varicourt, afterwards the wife of the Marquis de Villette, destined to become one of the heroes of the Jacobin club. For her he had a tender affection, which she warmly returned, and he gave her the pretty name 'Belle et Bonne' (beautiful and good) a title with which, through the rest of her life, her friends honoured her. This old man had ripened in the snows of Ferney into a singularly lovable character, and for miles around him the whole population looked to him as the author of its freedom and its happiness. One fancies, as he drove out to visit his mulberries and his horses, his silk-workers and his watchmakers, that he must often have said 'to the flying moment', like Faust among the multitude he had liberated from care, 'Ah! stay, thou art so fair.'

VIII

THE CALAS AFFAIR

In 1762, at Toulouse, an aged Protestant, Jean Calas, was executed with medieval barbarity. The charge against him was that he murdered his son, in order to prevent his conversion to the Catholic Church. In fact, the young man, who had no intention of changing his faith, took his own life. Few judicial crimes have had a profounder influence on history. It roused Voltaire to the supreme effort of his career. It excited in the French people, and far beyond the borders of France, an interest so lively that echoes of it were still audible thirty years afterwards, during the Revolution. It touched the popular imagination so profoundly that no less than eight plays were written about it. It was the Dreyfus case of the eighteenth century, and like that much more complicated affair it deepened the chasm that separated liberal France from the Catholic Church.

Toulouse had long been a focus of fanaticism. The savage crusade against the Albigenses left its memories. Rabelais's hero quitted its University, because it had a habit of 'roasting its professors like herring, his own blood being hot enough to need no further heating'. In 1562 there was a massacre of Protestants in the city, in which it is believed that about four thousand perished. A celebration of this exploit was held annually by the devout, but at each centenary the commemoration was exceptionally solemn and prolonged. In 1761 the Pope issued a Bull extending the privileges of the approaching festival to eight days. Even in 1862 it was still celebrated in the churches, though the Emperor forbade processions in the streets. In this town lived Jean Calas, a Huguenot draper, who enjoyed the respect of all who knew him. His eldest son, Marc-Antoine, was gifted and ambitious, had taken his bachelor's degree, had studied law and wished to enter this profession. But by the legislation of Louis XIV, no Protestant could enter any branch of the law: medicine was also closed, and even printers, jewellers, grocers and midwives had to give proof of orthodoxy. The required certificate of 'catholicity' was occasionally given in good-nature without much inquiry, but the young man was unable to qualify. He was a clever amateur actor, had some gift of eloquence, and thought for a moment of the Huguenot ministry, but found on reflection that he had no vocation for martyrdom. The 'pastors of the desert' were outlaws: to preach a sermon was a capital crime, and anyone who heard it was likely to be sent to the galleys (in Voltaire's phrase) for 'praying to God in bad French'. In this same year one of these ministers was hanged at Toulouse for exhorting, baptizing and marrying his flock. Such unions, one may add, had no legal validity: every Huguenot child was a bastard, and any heritage was assigned by the Courts to the nearest Catholic kinsman.

The young man, balked of a career, became moody and desperate and took to gambling. One evening in October 1761, a friend of the family named Lavaysse called at the Calas' house and stayed to supper. Mark rose after the meal and went out alone, as his custom was, while the rest of the family and their visitor sat talking. When he rose to go, the third son, Peter, saw him out. In the shop they found Mark's body hanging. They cut him down, called the family and a surgeon, and tried in vain to restore him. Meanwhile the watch had arrived; a crowd was gathering, and the rumour ran that old Calas had strangled Mark, to prevent his following the example of his second son Louis, who some time before this tragedy had turned Catholic. It was a popular belief that Huguenot parents were required by their Church in such cases to murder their offspring. The watch arrested the whole family, father, mother and son, together with the visitor and an elderly maid. On this charge of murder they were all now committed for trial. The Church had no hesitations. It took the dead heretic, Mark, to its bosom: the confraternities of Penitents were mobilized; processions of their members filled the streets, and with all the pomp and solemnity of the appropriate ritual Mark was buried as a martyr to the faith. Witnesses were ordered from every pulpit to come forward, under pain of excommunication. Even so, not a scrap of trustworthy evidence was gathered to suggest that Mark had shown any sign of quitting the religion of his family. In the first trial before the 'capitouls' (magistrates) one of their number was censured 'for partiality to the accused' and resigned, while the defending counsel was censured and suspended. The higher Court (Parlement) now took over the case, and before it the accused had no advocate. The judges were divided, at first seven and afterwards eight for conviction, five for acquittal. This majority sufficed. Jean Calas was sentenced to torture and death.

The old man's body was first tortured on the rack. The torment by pouring water into him followed. Then, half naked, with a rope round his neck, he was exposed before the Cathedral. Nothing was wrung from him but protestations of his innocence. He was then stretched on a wheel, and with eleven blows of an iron bar his limbs and ribs were broken. After two hours' exposure, he was strangled and his body burned. He bore himself bravely to the end, and died with the reminder that his Master, Jesus Christ, 'who was innocence itself', died a yet more cruel death.

The Parlement of Toulouse had no evidence, and had relied on extorting a confession from Jean Calas by torture. Failing in this, it now acquitted his widow, Lavaysse, and the maid. Peter was banished, as the vague sentence ran, 'in connection with the case'— which meant that there was no precise charge against him. He was, in fact, kidnapped and confined in a monastery and there more or less forcibly 'converted', but contrived to escape after four months. Two daughters, who were in the country on the day of Mark's death, were also shut up forcibly in monasteries. Friends helped the youngest boy, Donat, who also was in the country, to escape to Geneva.

There were in Geneva several citizens of some standing who had known Calas, and they endeavoured to interest Voltaire. At first he was puzzled, sceptical, but none the less moved. He wrote to leading men in the south of France, a Cardinal among them, for further facts. He questioned Donat, a boy of sixteen, for several days. He ascertained from several quarters, Catholic priests among them, that old Calas, so far from being a fanatic, was a man of unusual tolerance. He had shown no disapproval of Louis, when he went over to the Church. At length Peter, an eye-witness, also reached

Geneva, and Voltaire, after questioning him at length, lost all his doubts. The Parlement had acted with gross unreason. It was physically impossible that a feeble old man could have strangled Mark, a vigorous man in the prime of life, without assistance. Yet the only possible accomplices had been acquitted. If murder it was, then at least Lavaysse and Peter were equally guilty, and the mother and maid were accomplices. But the maid was an ardent Catholic, who had assisted in the conversion of Louis. Finally, a letter, written by Mark, was found, in which he blamed his brother severely for his conversion. In short, there was no occasion or motive for this supposed murder, which was physically and psychologically inconceivable, and no shred of evidence had been produced to support a baseless suspicion. The murderous fanatics were the clergy and judges of Toulouse.

Voltaire now put everything else aside to extort from Catholic France a reversal of this sentence. Through three years of incessant effort he sacrificed his leisure, his work, even his quarrels. He lived through these years, as he put it, ashamed if a random smile chanced to cross his lips. He spent his own money liberally, both to support the ruined Calas family, and to meet the monstrous costs of legal proceedings. He worked as a loyal comrade, and latterly as an affectionate friend, with a little group of Genevan Protestants, poles apart from him in their beliefs. He bestowed on the broken widow the most tactful and solicitous care. He wrote long and able memoranda for the lawyers, and a pamphlet for the public. In an incessant stream of letters, he roused every friend and acquaintance he could reach, not in France only, but in Europe. He interested the London Press, gathered subscriptions in England, and laid his philosophic kings under contribution. He roused the sympathies of great ladies of the Court, Mme de Pompadour among them, set the salons talking and the philosophers writing. With all this characteristic energy, he combined an astonishing tactical wisdom. He would allow no exaggerations, not even any general argument for toleration, until this test case were won. He bought up a rash book by a Protestant pastor, lest it should prejudice his appeal. The case, which needed skilful piloting, advanced very slowly, yet without a mishap. The Grand Council, with the King presiding in person, first moved for revision. A year later the sentences were quashed for reasons of form. Finally, before the King's Court of Appeal, three years to a day after the execution of Jean Calas, the case was re-tried; the defence was heard for the first time; all the accused, the dead and the living, were acquitted, and the Parlement of Toulouse was ordered to erase the record of its sentences. All these decisions were unanimous.

The effect of this campaign of Voltaire's was to lighten enor-mously, in actual practice, the load of oppression that lay on French Protestants. He alternately succeeded and failed in his efforts to get the 'convicts for faith' released from the galleys, but systematic toleration came only with the Revolution. No sooner was Calas vindicated than he had to throw himself into another similar affair. Sirven, a Protestant of a rather higher social status, escaped to Geneva while the other case was pending, though his elder daughter, who was with child, had died as they fled on foot across the Alps in winter. His younger daughter had been kidnapped and placed in a monastery (a common occurrence in this century) where physical ill-usage, designed to convert her, underminded her reason. Covered with bruises, she was sent home, and soon afterwards drowned herself in a well. Sirven was accused of murder, convicted in his absence, and executed in effigy. Voltaire, with wise generalship, postponed the appeal until the Calas case was finished: he then won it with less expenditure of effort than the first affair had cost him.

There soon followed, however, a still more horrible affair: intolerance had been defeated but not disarmed. A crucifix was mutilated at Abbeville, and suspicion fell on three very young men, one of them a mere lad. There was no evidence against them, but they had recently been seen to behave gracelessly in public: they had failed to uncover as the Host was carried past them in the street. They were ill-educated youths of what is called 'good' birth, who read freethinking books, Voltaire's among them, and talked rashly. One of them, Étallonde, escaped: the youngest, Moisnel, aged only seventeen, avowed everything required of him, under pressure, and accused his two friends, but afterwards withdrew both his extorted confession and his accusations. The Chevalier de la Barre, a spirited young man of twenty, remained firm under torture, but was convicted. An appeal to the Parlement of Paris failed by fifteen votes against ten, and the ghastly sentence was confirmed. De la Barre firmly refused to recite the confession prescribed to him, and resisted the executioner successfully when he tried to cut out his tongue. His head was then cut off and thrown into the flames, and with it a copy of Voltaire's *Philosophic Dictionary*. It is on record that the crowd applauded as the executioner tossed the lad's head into the fire.

This affair moved too swiftly for any effective intervention, nor was Voltaire an altogether disinterested spectator. Indeed, he felt himself in danger, and even thought for a time of migrating with his philosophic friends to Cleves in Prussian territory, where they should set up their 'factory of truth', by which he meant a free press. His duty to his colony kept him, however, at Ferney, and as usual, whatever his fears for his own safety, he went on with his campaign against superstition with more daring and fewer disguises than before. For Étallonde he obtained from Frederick a commission in the Prussian army, but failed in his efforts to get his capital sentence quashed.

It may be thought that Voltaire's motive in taking up these three affairs was his hostility to the Church. Doubtless he hated cruelty even more bitterly than usual when it was wrought in the name of a religion that preaches charity and mercy. But he would show the same hatred of injustice and the same detestation of cruelty in cases that had neither a religious nor a political interest. He took much trouble, in an ordinary criminal case, to save the life of a certain Madame Montbailly, and here he had time to prove her innocence with success, though her equally innocent husband had been executed. The law, brutal in all else, postponed her execution because she was with child. Voltaire was almost as keen to reform the barbarous legal procedure of his time, as he was to establish toleration, and all these affairs, in which the stupidity of the law was surpassed only by its cruelty, gave him his chance. This theme, in letters, pamphlets, tales and histories, runs persistently through his writings. He would bestir himself as readily for a foreigner as for a fellow-countryman. When in 1756 he read of the danger in which Admiral Byng stood for the loss of Minorca, he obtained from the

commander of the French fleet in this engagement, who happened
to be his lifelong friend, the Duc de Richelieu, a letter which paid a
chivalrous tribute to Byng's conduct. It had some effect on the
court-martial and won four votes for acquittal, while the majority
added to their verdict of guilty a recommendation to mercy which
the King chose to disregard. Byng was then shot, as Voltaire put it,
'to encourage the others'. A similar affair employed Voltaire's pen
in the last years of his life. Count Lally, a brilliant soldier of Irish
origin, was made a scapegoat by the French East India Company
for their reverses in that Peninsula, and after a long imprisonment
and a grossly unfair trial, he was executed. Voltaire took immense
pains to ascertain the historical facts and wrote a powerful vindication, while the dead man's son, Lally-Tollendal, pressed for a posthumous reversal of the dishonouring sentence. As Voltaire lay on
his death-bed, the news reached him that the same Grand Council
that had vindicated Calas had, at last, after fifteen years, rehabili-
tated Lally. After days of silent torpor he sat up, his eyes shining,
and dictated a few lines of congratulation to the son, which ended
with the words 'Now I die happy'. He then called for a sheet of
paper, and had inscribed on it this sentence: 'On 26th May the
judicial murder committed by Pasquier on the person of Lally was
avenged by the King's Council.' This paper he caused to be pinned
to the tapestry, and through what were left to him of conscious
hours, his eyes rested on it. Rarely in any age has there lived on this
earth a man possessed by this consuming and disinterested passion
for justice.

IX

ÉCRASEZ L'INFÂME

During the later period of Voltaire's life there appears with great frequency, in his letters to his friends, the motto: Écrasez l'infâme (Crush the infamous thing). The phrase can be traced to the years spent in Prussia, but it was during the Calas affair that it became the war-cry and password of the philosophic party. They used it almost as an act of ritual, and often substitute for it a contraction unintelligible to the profane. What was this infamous thing? A first rough answer to this question is easy. L'infâme was the accursed power that had bound Calas to a wheel and broken his limbs. It was the power that had tossed the spirited head of young De la Barre into the flames, and thrown the *Philosophic Dictionary* after it. It was the dark force, as stupid as it was cruel, that had robbed France of the hands and brains of half a million industrious Huguenots. It was a power with a venerable history behind it, yet still it lived in this happy century of enlightenment, rabid in Toulouse, brutal in Abbeville, and firmly entrenched in the highest law court of the capital. Call it, as you please, intolerance or superstition: every philosopher knew what it meant. It had dogged him through all his years of mental life. It burned his books. It imposed on him constant resort to humiliating subterfuges and disguises. It stood over him with the perpetual threat of exile or prison. The time had come, Voltaire felt, to make an end. The Calas affair had given him hope, while the judicial atrocity at Abbeville had warned him of his danger. He had had enough of sapping and mining: he would rely no longer on irony and suggestion: it shall be a frontal attack. The infamous thing must be crushed.

The objective of the campaign was at first defined in surprisingly moderate terms. In 1760, two years before the Calas affair, he wrote to D'Alembert: 'I want you to crush the infamous thing: that's the great point. It must be reduced to the state in which it is in England,

and you will succeed if you choose. That is the greatest service one could render to the human race.' In this letter it is obvious that L'Infâme has a rather more definite meaning than superstition or intolerance. It seems to be not supernatural religion, or even the Catholic Church: what it meant was apparently the ecclesiastical power, or possibly this power in its coercive aspect. England had her Established Church, but as Voltaire insists in the *Letters* it was subject to Parliament: heretics and nonconformists were denied the full, active rights of citizenship, but they were free to utter and print their thoughts. To ask for no more than this was to make a modest demand, yet even this minimum meant a sweeping transformation in French life. Toleration was certainly the effect at which Voltaire aimed, but his study of history, no less than his experience of the complicated religious disputes of his own lifetime over the Jansenist heresy, had taught him to see in this issue something more fundamental than the abstract right to worship or debate with freedom. The root of the matter for him was the relationship of the secular to the ecclesiastical power. That was what had been settled once for all in England at the Reformation. The problem could be approached from either end. One could state the case for toleration on its merits: one could expose the brutalities and follies of intolerance. This Voltaire did, but he never lost sight of the central objective, the chaining up of the ecclesiastical power. His aim, in short, was to disarm the Church, to end Theocracy.

The more immediate task he undertook in his *Treatise on Tolerance*, which sprang hot from the Calas affair. The first draft of it was already circulating in manuscript in 1763. He begins with a moving and persuasive narrative of the case, and from this starting-point, that touched the best instincts of humanity, opens out his broader argument. Voltaire had in perfection the gift of using a contemporary event to set men thinking. What he had done with the disaster of Lisbon he now did again. He passes easily from the sufferings of this innocent Huguenot to an account of the motives that underlay the schisms of the Reformation, and in so doing he contrives to suggest that the attitude of the Protestants was not surprisingly different from that of the average French Catholic layman of his own day, who also grudged the tribute and the

obedience that a foreign Power exacted. He laughs at the suggestion
that tolerance might endanger the peace of the realm. It is true that
the Huguenots revolted in the past: but will gentleness cause
revolts, as cruelty did? He dwells on the losses that France sustained by the Huguenot emigration—a diminished population, the
decay of many industries, the reinforcement of the armies of her
enemies. He next embarks on a much bolder line of argument. He
maintains, with truth, that classical antiquity was on the whole
tolerant. He minimizes the persecutions that the early Christians
endured, and disposes of many of the legends of the martyrs as incredible. With a rather risky use of his habitual irony, he argues
that to go on recounting false and ridiculous wonders must weaken
that faith that we owe to true miracles. He contrives, as he goes
along, to remind Catholics of their own record of barbarism, the
massacre of St. Bartholomew and the savageries of Louis XIV
against the Protestants of the Cevennes. He even argues that the
ancient Jews were tolerant, and disposes of the Gospel texts,
especially 'Compel them to come in', which the Church used to
justify persecution. He fills a chapter with quotations from the
Fathers and from modern Bishops that point in the direction of
tolerance. He uses, skilfully enough, the general weariness that
average Frenchmen felt, after the interminable controversies of
Jansenists and Jesuits, to excite an active disgust at the excesses of
both parties. He describes the scenes that went on round the death-
bed of persons suspected of some barely intelligible heresy, as the
confessor doled out tickets for the next world. He recounts the
quarrels of Christian missionaries that closed China to the Gospel.
He tries to drive a wedge between the monastic Orders, whom he
execrates, and the secular clergy, whom he will flatter mildly.
He concludes with some chapters that stand out among the most
brilliant things he ever wrote. With a wit and humanity that
never flag, he argues that dogma is of no consequence and social
morality all-important. He ends with a plea that we should regard
all men, be they Protestants or Moslems, as our brothers, and
clinches his argument with an irresistible use of his gift of dramatic irony—a scene in which he represents a just God damning
to all eternity the most virtuous men of antiquity, while he

admits to Paradise the assassins and fanatics reared in the true faith.

One may truly say of this book, as solemn critics have said, that it does not rank with the work of Locke, or with Mill *On Liberty*. It is not a philosophical treatise. It is a pamphlet of genius addressed to the average men of Voltaire's own day. It condescends to address them on their own level. It quotes the Fathers of the Church. It makes use of the lingering belief that antiquity, or at all events classical antiquity, was incomparably superior to this modern age in wisdom. It contrives, without alarming the typical layman, who is not ready to break dramatically with the Church, to suggest to him what is in effect the Deist attitude. One could not in this way train martyrs for free thought, or drill its adherents to advance as shock troops upon the enemy. That was not Voltaire's purpose. What one could achieve by such a book was rather to foster a kindly, indulgent attitude towards Huguenots and other eccentrics who held unusual beliefs; to arouse a civilian vigilance against frocked fanatics; to turn men's minds away from every form of Other-Worldliness; to break the barriers that faith had raised against the majority of mankind. With all respect for Locke and Mill, one may doubt whether they achieved any result as considerable as this. On the whole, Voltaire did achieve it, for this was the attitude that he and his philosophic generation stamped upon French civilization. It is, at home, the attitude of the liberal Republic; in Asia and Africa it makes for social relations, when Frenchmen find themselves among Buddhists or Mahommedans, rather easier, rather more kindly and equal, than obtain in the dependencies of other European Powers.

The *Treatise* did not concern itself with the legal or constitutional definition of toleration: it is content to say that the State should punish nothing save actual physical attacks by fanatics on other creeds. The *Dictionary*, on the other hand, contains a page, drafted with not a little precision, which sums up the urgent reforms that Voltaire thought it timely to demand. This astonishing medley was probably the most widely read of all Voltaire's works. The idea of it arose in the debates of King Frederick's Round Table, but it was not published till 1764, in a form known as the 'portable' or pocket *Philosophic Dictionary*. It contains, in the alphabetical order of their subjects, a series of essays, none of them lengthy and some of them very brief, on most of the opinions that Voltaire held tenaciously and on some of his crotchets. Occasionally a dialogue is substituted for a disquisition, and the style is always lively and popular and often amusing. Among the subjects figure some of the graver themes that all philosophic systems have discussed—liberty, the nature of the soul, the existence of God. There are arresting political essays on war, inequality, tyrants and toleration. Doubt is cast on the existence of Moses and the authorship of the Pentateuch, and there are lively comments on the moral conduct of Abraham and other Biblical heroes. With these brief, entertaining articles Voltaire must have reached, as the years went on, literally, millions of readers who would not have applied themselves to a long book that called for sustained attention. The *Dictionary* became, through a great part of the nineteenth century, the bible of the liberal middle class in France, which often described itself as 'Voltairian'. The items in this particular article on 'Laws, Civil and Ecclesiastical', made their appearance in most of the 'cahiers' of the Third Estate on the eve of the Revolution. They form an extremely moderate but still valuable programme, the basis of that idea of a secular State which French liberalism finally realized after the Dreyfus Affair—for one may say that the effort to laicize the State began with the martyrdom of Jean Calas and ended with the vindication of Alfred Dreyfus. Voltaire does not here ask for lay education, or for the expulsion and expropriation of the monastic congregations, though elsewhere he does suggest that monasteries be turned into asylums for the aged. His list of urgent reforms is interesting, since it shows us precisely where the Church had made its tyranny insufferable to lay common sense. The principle laid down in the first clause is that 'no ecclesiastical law shall be enforced until it has received the express sanction of the civil government'. There follow several clauses that disclose some of the outstanding grievances of the time. Marriage shall be a civil contract: the priest may bless it, but no more. The Church shall not interfere with loans at interest—one of the basic causes of the Reformation. Ecclesiastics shall be subject to the civil courts, and shall no longer be exempt from taxation. Their right to forbid work on Saints' days shall be taken from them. Nor shall any right of a citizen be at their mercy, if they choose to brand him as a sinner—a reference among other things to their power to deny decent burial to actors, free-thinkers and heretics no less than 'sinners'. And once more we en-counter that bitter economic grievance of the thrifty Gallican patriot —the 'annates', the payment to Rome of the first year's revenues of every newly-appointed bishop. These, then, were the places where the yoke galled. It is not always the worst wrongs that make a decisive break in history. Voltaire knew his fellow-countrymen: for his own part he had weightier reasons than these for his deter-mination to crush the infamous thing.

His real mind is disclosed in the *Essay on Customs*, the arsenal that contained the heavy artillery for this campaign. One soon realizes that underneath the ambition to trace through the centuries the progress of the human mind, another purpose is at work. Voltaire is engaged upon the natural history of supernatural religion, and inevitably the chief subject of his researches is Christianity, and more specifically the Catholic Church. He is concerned with it primarily as a system of dogma based on revelation and the authority of an infallible Church. Of a specifically Christian morality he has little to say, since his general position is that the essentials of morality are common to all peoples and all religions: certainly he has no criticisms to offer. His references to the founder of Christi-anity are invariably inspired by the deepest respect, though a denial of His divinity is, of course, a central tenet of his Deism. One may describe the whole serried argument, the sustained, pitiless narrative, as an assault by a moralist on theology and its fruits. He starts with the assumption that religions were founded to inculcate morality, and his continual refrain is that they have poisoned the life of man-kind because they neglected ethics for dogma. He explores, as he goes along, at first with an ironical bow to the truth of the Catholic religion, the means to which the Church was driven to establish its authority. The Old Testament is subjected to a terrific assault, on the double ground that its miraculous history is incredible, and that these tales, if true, would be an abominable slander on the goodness of God. Voltaire was moved to a horror and indignation that he was never weary of expressing by the cruelties of God's chosen people, and he even troubled to write a ghastly little tragedy, *Saul*, which is a mosaic of texts, lifted literally from the Scriptures, narrating the crimes of David and his family. Readers who were themselves brought up on the Bible can understand his feelings: an emancipated generation will marvel at his passion and pertinacity. Voltaire's handling of miracles is masterly. He makes no frontal attack on those which Faith requires us to accept, but he singles out from classical antiquity analogous wonders which we are free to reject. The parallel is amusingly effective. No miracles were ever better attested than the cures publicly wrought by Vespasian, yet no one credits them, 'since in this case there was no one who had an interest in sustaining belief'. His directest thrust is in the passages that call attention to the astonishing silence of all contemporary witnesses to the Plagues of Egypt and the convulsions of Nature that attended the Crucifixion. 'These it was the province of the Holy Spirit alone to relate: God did not wish that a history so divine should be transmitted to us by any profane hand.' He has many diverting pages on the miracles of the Church, which grew less frequent as academies of science were established. But he spares none of the foundations on which the authority of the Church reposed—the supposed prophecies, the invented verses of the Sibyl, the play on words that justified the claims of the Papacy, the forged Decretals. Some instructive pages trace the gradual evolution of the sacraments of the Church. Voltaire narrates the unedifying history of the Councils, Nicæa, Constance and Trent, that established the essentials of the Faith, the two latter in careful detail. One makes at Constance the closer acquaintance of Pope John XXIII, who bought with his gains as a pirate his Cardinal's hat and another man's wife, while at Trent the final definition of orthodox belief was fixed by the intrigues of Pope Paul III to find a duchy for his bastard. One is compelled to realize the accidents of force, fraud and personal ambition that accounted for the selection of the articles of belief on which our eternal salvation depends. The ironical disguises of the earlier chapters vanish as we proceed, and at length Voltaire flings all restraint away with a terrific rhetorical assault upon the Papacy: 'at once the scandal, the terror, and the

divinity of European Catholics.' This, then, is his verdict on theocracy: 'the more this system of government claimed to be divine,
the more abominable it was.'

The main burden of the indictment has yet to come. Voltaire
describes 'l'Infâme' in action. With patient industry he recounts
for us the cruelty and rapacity of the Eastern Crusades, the savagery
of the Holy War against the most sympathetic of medieval heretics,
the Albigenses, the treacherous burning of Hus, the horrors of the
Spanish Inquisition, the civil wars of religion in France and the
thirty years war of religion that all but extinguished civilization in
Germany. If in the *Century* he had exercised some restraint in
describing the pious cruelties of Louis XIV, he shows no mercy
to him in the *Essay*. The case against Protestant intolerance occu-
pies less space, but Calvin emerges from the devout murder of
Servetus an execrable figure; he tells the ghastly story of Henry
VIII's public debate with the Baptist Lambert, which ended with
that heretic's execution; nor does he forget Cromwell's cruelties in
Ireland. Interwoven with this record of holy wars and persecutions
is a close narrative of the anarchy caused by the pretensions to
supremacy of the ecclesiastical over the civil power, and of the repeated assassinations to which in the seventeenth century it led.
Voltaire lived in the past as intensely as in the present—indeed,
he says in one of his letters that every year, on the anniversary of St.
Bartholomew, he suffered from a feverish attack. The *Essay* has the
power of an experience through which the author has lived. There
is in this narrative of the fruits of fanaticism none of the graceful
levity of the early chapters. It has all been felt; one is scorched
by this record, and few readers, one supposes, could follow it to the
end without joining in the cry: écrasez l'Infâme. The whole mis-
chief, he concludes, flowed from this: 'that authority bade men believe, instead of telling them to be just.'

On this great book rests the chief claim of Voltaire to the gratitude of humanity. If we in this age are slow to recognize it, it is
because it had done its work before we knew this earth. In the
Essay and the innumerable popular pamphlets on miracles and the
scriptures that came after it, he and his school broke the belief in a
literally inspired revelation, turned the miracles that were the

Church's title to our obedience into an embarrassing inheritance, destroyed the empire of dogma and compelled the churches to survive by anything rather than the old theocratic claim. They live on by preaching, with many reservations, the Sermon on the Mount: they console us with a Heaven open wide to all the children of men: they 'interpret' science and 'reconcile' themselves to its conclusions; they even organize their world-congresses of all the faiths, at which, in charitable discussion with rabbis, brahmins and imams, they search for that 'natural religion' which Voltaire preached. But it is the way of the world, when it has reluctantly learned its lesson from a daring pioneer, to retain the horror with which it first regarded him. Wit is an alarming tool, for most of us are mental cowards.

For the rest, the grounds on which a modern historian would modify Voltaire's indictment of 'l'Infâme' do not restore its reputation. He was careful over facts: the slips inevitable in a book of this scope and length are neither numerous nor serious. A Catholic historian may fairly stress some considerations that he stated too briefly. He may have exaggerated somewhat the part played by monasticism and theological feuds in weakening the defences of the Roman Empire against the barbarians. On the other hand, he dwells too lightly on the slow but thorough work of a religion, as intolerant as it was other-worldly, in destroying the free intellectual life of antiquity. The closing of the Athenian Schools of Philosophy dates the triumph of the Church, but on this day civilization sustained the deadliest defeat in its history. Voltaire is too harsh in his judgement of the monastic orders, 'within which men swear to God to live at the expense of others and to be useless'. He does, indeed, recognize both their charitable works and their services in conserving some remnants of learning through the Dark Ages, but these admissions hardly soften his total condemnation of 'these eternal families that perpetuate themselves at the expense of all the rest'. He struggles, indeed, to be fair, as in the passage in which he eulogizes the austere lives of the Calvanist pastors, who took nothing for themselves from the loot of the Church's riches: 'they sounded the charge, but never shared the spoil.' But what historian, with the passions of a man, could achieve impartiality in such an argument as this? The main qualification, however, that forces itself on our minds is one that Voltaire himself suggests on every other page. Were dogma and fanaticism really the exciting causes of all these cruelties and oppressions, or were the dogmas rather the symbols in a savage war of classes, in which the authority of the Catholic Church came to the aid of the defenders of economic privilege and the older order of society?

The chief advantage that our generation enjoys over Voltaire's, in estimating the part that religion played in the development of civilization, comes from our greater familiarity with pre-history and anthropology. It was his distinction that he knew that every great issue of human society has its roots in the dim past. He rightly guessed that theocracy originated in the earliest civilizations of the East. This issue arose round the Pyramids: he meant to end it at Ferney. But like all the 'philosophers', Voltaire was inclined to dwell on the swollen power of priestly castes, without understanding the part they played in the daily life, even the economic life of early civilizations. All of them were grouped round a divine king, at once god incarnate and priest of his own cult. On him it fell to perform the rites that ensured the orderly procession of the seasons. To the motions of his ritual marched the stars, and only when he drove the plough through the first furrow was it certain that harvest would follow seedtime. In his hands lay economic power, for he controlled the rains, and on his virility depended the fertility of seeds and the multiplication of flocks and herds. The political history of mankind begins with the gradual division and specialization of the functions at first united in this king-god. Below him, incomparably less sacred and august, arose the war-king, and an inevitable rivalry declared itself. Priest-king and war-king reigned side by side in uneasy dualism. Voltaire noted this phase in the Japan of his day: it has survived down to our own time in some islands of the Pacific. It is a division of powers so natural, nay so inevitable for primitive thought, that it reproduced itself, when the classical civilization disappeared, in the age-long quarrel between Empire and Papacy, the civil power and the Church. This background to his theme Voltaire dimly discerned. Groping, however, among origins imperfectly understood, he started from an assumption that vitiated part of his interpretation of early history. He supposed that all religions were instituted to support morality. Early forms of religion had no relation whatever to morals, and any bearing they had on conduct derived from ritual and ceremonial. It was only after a long and difficult evolution that the human conscience came to draw, one might almost say extort, from religions built up to serve wholly different ends, some sanction and support for a social morality. This Voltaire could not know. Nor could he guess that the pattern of Christian legend itself was shaped by age-long memories of the divine king slain to fertilize the fields.

A friend of Voltaire's after reading his record of the doings of l'infâme, asked of him, since he had destroyed supernatural religion, what he offered in its place. 'What!' he answered, 'I rid you of a wild beast, and you ask me what I would put in its place.' None the less he had his definite creed of Natural Religion. It is a mistake to rank Voltaire among the original thinkers who added something of their own to metaphysical thought. He made no such pretensions. 'Philosophy', as he understood it, was an attitude of mind rather than a system. He had read Locke and Berkeley, Descartes, Malebranche and Leibnitz, and was content to count himself the grateful pupil of the first of these thinkers. He wrote early in the Cirey period (about 1734), for the benefit of Madame du Châtelet, a brief and sparkling essay that bears the too ambitious title *Treatise on Metaphysics*, but was never published during his lifetime. This, with his didactic poems and some articles in the *Dictionary*, was his only attempt to expound his beliefs in an orderly and positive form. One need not follow his reasoning in any detail: the results alone are important. He accepted without modification Locke's analysis of the process of knowledge, with him rejected innate ideas, and derived all experience from the impressions of the senses. He was firmly persuaded of the existence of God, the Creator. The reasoning that led him to reject the hypothesis of a self-sufficient Universe, existing in its own right from the beginning, was purely scholastic. He started by making an absolute separation between matter and motion, and when once he had made this abstraction he could not bring them together, save with the aid of a First Cause.

Commonly he was content to beg the whole question of Creation in metaphors. 'I shall always be convinced,' he wrote in a letter of 1741, 'that a watch proves a watchmaker, and that a universe proves a God.' That his Deism was a deep and sincere conviction one cannot doubt, but one has some difficulty in grasping his conception of the Deity. In his earlier writings one strives to imagine a sublime and eternal maker of mathematical instruments, a more venerable Robert Boyle, an immortal Huygens, who devised and wound up that vast mechanism of incomparable precision that we call the Universe.

When Voltaire turned to the proper study of mankind, he found himself wholly unable to give any definite meaning to the idea of the soul, and he questioned whether philosophy would ever probe the secret. He tells us that true philosophy consists in knowing where to stop. In this chapter he is on his guard against the process of abstraction, and will not separate matter and thought, as he had separated matter and motion. God organized our bodies to think, precisely as he organized them to eat and digest. The heavy balance of probability is, therefore, against the immortality of the soul, though he will not deny it with dogmatic confidence.

The freedom of the will he denies in the scholastic sense of liberty of indifference, but to liberty he none the less gives some meaning. A completely enlightened being is free: liberty is the health of the soul. Morals have a meaning only in society. Virtue and vice, moral good and evil, is, then, in every country, what is useful or harmful to society. There is nothing absolutely and in itself good or evil—no categorical imperative, to use Kant's terminology. Everything changes with circumstance: a lie in certain conditions may be an act of heroism. God gave us no revelation to disclose his laws to us. Let us be content with the gifts he did bestow—reason, self-love, benevolence towards our kind, our needs, our passions, the means in short by which we have built up society. 'These who need the help of religion to be good men are to be pitied. They must be social monsters, if they fail to find in themselves the sentiments necessary to that society, and are obliged to borrow elsewhere what ought to exist in their own nature.'

To this utilitarian and social view of morals Voltaire adhered to the end. But one notes some developments in his thinking. In his poem on *Natural Law* he expounds a doctrine of conscience. His psychology is rudimentary, and he does not inquire by what sub-conscious processes our intuitive and quasi-instinctive judgements on conduct are formed. He insists that such moral judgements are not to be confused with those we make upon external matters and accept from our parents and the society round us. There is a natural law that has been impressed on our minds by God. True, it does not speak to us in infancy. It must mature in us with time, and be strengthened by use. It is not easy to give precision to Voltaire's thought; he seems to be bringing back innate ideas under another name: but broadly his meaning is clear enough. These implanted dictates of conscience constitute the simple principles of social con-duct that all the tribes of men must follow, however various their beliefs, their circumstances and their level of civilization.

Finally, there emerges in Voltaire's later writings a statement of Deism and a conception of God that differ widely from what one took to be his early view. God is now for him much more than a Creator, a First Cause. He is goodness and justice itself: He stands in some direct relationship to men: He has planted in their minds the first principles of morality: in some way that we fail to understand, He rewards virtuous and punishes evil conduct. This happens, apparently in this life, for though the Chinese sage in the Diction-ary (catéchisme chinois) affirms a belief in immortality, Voltaire in one of his later letters to Frederick still doubts it. This state of mind, in which faith and resignation battle with bewilderment, is that of the Poem on the Disaster at Lisbon.

The clearest affirmation—one cannot call it an explanation—is to be found under 'Théisme' and 'Théiste' in the big *Philosophic Dictionary*—the seven volumes of miscellaneous essays and frag-ments compiled by his editors after his death. Here he says plainly that to consider God simply as a creator who has made admirable machines is not religion. That begins when one realizes that 'God has designed to make a relationship between Himself and men'. . . . 'He is a true Theist who says to God: "I adore Thee and serve Thee," and to the Turk, the Chinese, the Indian and the Russian, "I love you" . . . The Theist is firmly persuaded of the existence of a supreme Being as good as He is powerful, who formed all extended beings, perpetuates their kinds, punishes crime without cruelty, and recompenses virtuous actions with bounty. The Theist does not know how God punishes, or how He favours and pardons, and is not rash enough to flatter himself that he knows how God acts, but that God acts and that He is just, this he knows. The difficulties that tell against the idea of Providence do not shake his faith, because they are merely difficulties, and not demonstrations. . . . He is submissive to Providence, and . . . believes that it extends to all places and all centuries. . . . To do good is his worship, to submit to God his doctrine.'

Evidently one can advance no further in penetrating this mystery. One can, however, guess why Voltaire adopted this belief. He evidently grew doubtful of the position he took up at the close of the Treatise—that it is enough that we should know good from evil. He moved towards a pragmatist attitude, and perceived that a belief in divine rewards and punishments is useful to society and to princes. One reflects that the society of his day, and for that matter of ours, which seemed to require this external support, was in itself excessively imperfect. One can be moral only in a true society. But is moral conduct attainable, where, as he tells us, there is always a division between the oppressors and the oppressed, while the many, if they are to work for the benefit of the few, must be kept poor but not wretched? In a society ordered with less respect for class and more for equality, it is conceivable that moral conduct would seem so natural that men might dispense with the rewards and penalties of theism.

X

THE END

At last the tranquil years at Ferney drew to an end. At 84 Voltaire showed few signs of old-age, save a growing obstinacy. He worked with all his customary industry and method: his wit, his intellectual powers and his zest in life were unimpaired. There was, however, some decline in his creative imagination. His last tragedy, *Irène*, and his tale, *The Princess of Babylon*, are below his own high level. 'One might have taken him for an immortal,' wrote Condorcet, after a visit to Ferney in 1770, 'had not a trace of injustice towards Rousseau, and an excessive sensibility to the stupidities of Fréron led one to perceive that he is a man.' He was ideally happy at Ferney, but one wish haunted him—to see Paris again. It proved irresistible, as he finished his last play. He mistook it for his best work, and wanted above all things to see it worthily acted. Louis XV, whom neither Mme de Pompadour nor Mme du Barry, nor any of his ministers could ever induce to lift his veto on Voltaire's entry into the capital, was out of the way. Louis XVI was equally prejudiced, but less autocratic.

So to Paris in his carriage, still polishing the manuscript of his tragedy as he drove, Voltaire set out in the first days of February, 1778. His journey was a triumphal procession. Crowds thronged him wherever he was recognized. At Dijon some of the most distinguished young men of the town dressed themselves as waiters that they might have the honour of serving him at table in his hotel, and he was serenaded as he went to bed. He reached Paris in high spirits. 'I'm the only article of contraband here,' he said to the customs officers at the barrier, as they came out to search his carriage. He stayed with his beloved adopted daughter, Belle et Bonne, now the Marquise de Villette. In her drawing-room, day after day, the old man held a species of court, attired in his famous dressing-gown and night-cap, and half Paris came to welcome him.

He met again the two best friends of his youth, d'Argental and Richelieu, both of them octogenarians. The Academy sent a deputation to greet its most distinguished member. Benjamin Franklin called, bringing his grandson with him. At first they conversed in English, till Mme Denis reminded him that the company would like to follow their talk. 'Forgive me,' he said with his usual graciousness, 'if I yielded for a moment to the vanity of speaking the same language as Mr. Franklin.' The American philosopher begged the patriarch to give his blessing to his grandson. He laid his hands on the boy's head with the words, 'God and Liberty.'

When he called on Turgot, now out of office and under a cloud, he insisted on kissing that statesman's hands. When the younger man protested, Voltaire persisted: 'Let me kiss the hands that have signed the salvation of the people.' Then, as they talked and joked, he told Turgot, who was a martyr to gout, that he reminded him of Nebuchadnezzar's image. 'Yes,' said Turgot, 'my feet of clay.' 'Your head of gold,' answered Voltaire. One meets this unusual man as it were in the round in this anecdote. One feels the depth and sincerity of this passion for the well-being of the people that could prompt him in the hour of his own triumph to pay this act of homage to a defeated junior. Then, after this tense moment of emotion comes his fun, but what a gracious and flattering joke it was! The current notion of Voltaire is that his was a cold, glittering intellect that wielded a deadly and malicious wit. He was, in fact, an intensely emotional man, who always felt strongly, sometimes in anger, sometimes in sympathy and goodwill. As for his wit, it was a perfectly tempered tool that obeyed with instant precision the purpose of the hand that held it. It will serve him equally well to caress with exquisite grace an old friend or a charming woman, or with the same refined economy in movement to run an enemy through. The same artist is evident in both these operations, and in both we admire his consummate control over the most sensitive of European languages. But one is tempted to wager that an even ampler collection could be made of his gracious speeches that ring like music, than of his malicious thrusts.

The strain of all this excitement, after the tranquillity of Ferney, was too much, more especially as Voltaire insisted on answering every letter and returning every call. His physician issued the first of many warnings, There now reached him a simple letter from an unknown priest, Father Gaultier, an ex-Jesuit who was chaplain to the hospital for incurables, with a reminder that his immortal soul might soon be judged for all its actions, and an offer of his services. Voltaire was evidently touched. 'Your letter,' he answered, 'seems to be that of a good man.' After quoting his motto, 'God and Liberty', he went on: 'I am eighty-four: I shall soon appear before God the creator. If you have anything to say, it is my duty to receive your visit.' There was evidently some competition among the priests of Paris for the distinction of confessing the Arch-Deist on his death-bed. A certain Father Marthe had rushed in and summoned him imperiously to confess. 'From whom,' asked Voltaire, 'do you come?' 'From God,' was the answer. When Voltaire invited the intruder to show his credentials, he was nonplussed and withdrew. The parish priest of Saint-Sulpice considered that he alone was the official competent to issue a valid ticket to the next world, though one might have thought that the chaplain of the incurables was peculiarly suited to this difficult soul. His professional jealousy, as we shall see, wrecked a promising enterprise.

Gaultier called, on receiving this encouraging reply. They talked in private, and evidently Voltaire, who had in private life a curious sympathy with Jesuits, liked the man. Four days later he became seriously ill, and a hæmorrhage started which continued for three weeks. He now sent for Gaultier, and had to receive also a formal call from the parish priest. On March 2nd, he wished to confess. Gaultier, who meanwhile had received the instructions of the Archbiship, required a retractation. Voltaire wrote with his own hand: ' I die in the Catholic religion, in which I was born, hoping for the divine mercy, and the forgiveness of all my sins, and if ever I have scandalized the Church, I crave pardon of it and of God.' On this Gaultier was apparently willing to grant absolution and to give him the last sacrament, but Voltaire excused himself on the curious ground that he was spitting blood and might defile the wafer. Next day, Gaultier, after seeing the Archbishop, called again to explain that the retractation was insufficient, but found Voltaire unwilling to see him. From the date of the retractation his health

began to mend. Beyond an exchange of polite letters with the curé
and a formal call from him, nothing further happened in this matter
till the end of May.

What are we to make of this puzzling affair? In the first place it is
clear that Voltaire was in full possession of his faculties, and acted
deliberately. In the second place, it is equally clear that there was no
change in his opinions, and no wavering or fear in his own mind.
To his secretary, by birth a Protestant, who was shocked by these
comprises, he gave on February 28th a signed statement that ex-
pressed his real mind: 'I die adoring God, loving my friends, with
no hatred towards my enemies, and detesting superstition.' The
last word had in Voltaire's vocabulary a perfectly definite meaning.
It covered every form of religion, save 'natural' religion. It included
every form of Christianity, save perhaps Unitarianism, if that be
Christianity. Voltaire died, as he had lived, rejecting supernatural
religion.

One simple reason explains this tactical surrender. He had an
exaggerated dread of being 'thrown into a ditch'. He cared nothing
for Christian burial, but he did care intensely that his dead body
should be treated with respect. That this was his motive appears in
the contemporary statements of all his friends, several of whom
quote him. Of this not very philosophical fear of being buried like a
dog there are many traces in his writings, from the poem on
Adrienne Lecouvreur down to *Candide*. As usual, he took without
hesitation the direct means to achieve his end. The only way in those
days to be buried with decency was to grovel before a priest.
Voltaire accordingly did it, not for the first time. On at least three
occasions in his mature life, he performed the minimum act of conformity demanded by the Church; that is to say, in the usual
French phrase, he 'made his Easter'. He confessed and communicated on this greatest of the annual feasts, once at Colmar and twice
at Ferney. In our relatively free century, one reads of these dis-
honest and cowardly acts with shame and bewilderment. They were
unworthy of all that was great in Voltaire. This man was vain, yet
he had no conception of the place he would hold in the regard of
free men in days to come. Had he foreseen it, he would have preferred to their distress the meanest of ditches for his senseless bones.

Yet when this is said, it is proper to view his act in the light of history. He consulted his philosophic friends before he performed this insincere and unavailing act of conformity. Even D'Alembert, usually a severe moralist, approved. Other eminent men of his opinions, Fontenelle, Montesquieu, and Buffon did, or were soon to do the same thing. One must not suppose that this sacrament could have for Frenchmen in this century the solemnity that it possesses for our freer generation. Voltaire from his childhood had seen the sacrifice of the Mass performed, as often as not, by libertine and freethinking priests, who laughed at what they did. Round him were hundreds of thousands of men, some of them Huguenots on 364 days of the year, others convinced Deists, others merely indifferent, who gave this necessary proof of 'catholicity' once a year, since without it they could neither have earned their bread, nor held any respected position in society. A Church which persecutes must pay the price in the corruption of a nation's sincerity and self-respect. Christians have the right to condemn Voltaire's weakness, on one condition. Will they condemn with equal severity the brutality of a Christian Church that would allow a great citizen and a noble intellect to rank at death above the dogs, only by inflicting on him the shame of an acted lie?

Irène, meanwhile, had been performed with immense success, while its author lay in bed. Paris was too proud of the veteran to be critical. Night after night the theatre was thronged, and with the exception of the King, even the royal family attended, led by Marie Antoinette, who was friendly to Voltaire and would have received him, had not Louis XVI expressly forbidden her. The invalid was now sufficiently recovered to go about, and March the 30th, when he attended a sitting of the Academy in the afternoon, and went to the theatre in the evening, ranks as the supreme day of triumph in his career. Vast crowds thronged the streets whenever he went out, to catch a glimpse of him, and his carriage could hardly penetrate them, for the people climbed upon it and insisted on kissing his horses, if they could not reach his hands. A woman in the crowd was heard to say, 'It's M. de Voltaire, the defender of the oppressed, he who saved the families of Calas and Sirven.' Nowhere but in France would a poet have enjoyed a triumph that few conquerors have experienced. But these crowds were thinking of other claims to their gratitude than his tragedies. They doubtless felt the affection that human nature never refuses to a splendid old man. They rejoiced that their city should see him again after an exile of twenty-eight years. They remembered his good deeds to Sirven, the family of Calas and the peasants of Gex. But above all, they were saluting in him the patriarch of the philosophic Opposition. To applaud Voltaire was to demonstrate also against the Court that had banished him, and the Church to which his whole career was a challenge. A shrewd observer, had there been one among the writers of the police reports, might have based on these scenes a prediction of the coming revolution. In fact, the conservatives were alarmed. They hunted for the decree that had banished him, only to discover that there was no formal sentence, nothing but Louis XV's obstinate will. A few days after these manifestations, a Court chaplain, a certain Abbé de Beauregard, preached before the King a furious attack on the 'philosophers', which contained this ominous sentence: 'They accuse us of intolerance. Do they not know that charity has its fury and zeal its vengeance?' But the time for the exercise of these Christian virtues had not yet come.

The Academy broke all its customs to honour Voltaire, though its numerous clerical members absented themselves. The Immortals filed before him, made him the director of their work for the coming quarter, and then applauded an address by D'Alembert that contained an eloquent eulogy of Voltaire's poetical work. At the theatre, the little wizened figure appeared in his famous *perruque* in the style of forty years ago, and for twenty minutes the whole audience abandoned itself to a delirium of applause, while he was thrice crowned with laurel in his box. At the end of his tragedy, an actress thought of fetching Pigalle's bust from the lobby, and the whole cast improvised on the stage a solemn coronation, while the Empress Irène (Mme Vestris) twice recited a poem that promised Voltaire immortality in the name of France. Not less significant was the ceremony held a few days later at the masonic lodge of the Nine Sisters, to which belonged most of the liberal servants of the Muses in Paris, writers, painters and musicians. The lodges of the Grand Orient had become by this time the organized vanguard of militant, philosophic liberalism, French in its culture, international in its range. Into it the old man was initiated, and a symphony was played by the musical brethren. He was girt with the apron that Helvétius had worn, and he gave his ceremonial gloves to Belle et Bonne. The venerable brother who received him (Lalande, the astronomer), after dwelling on what he had done for his colony of refugees at Ferney, declared that he was already 'a mason by his actions', for he had 'rendered fanaticism odious and superstition ridiculous.'

In the last days of April, after another triumphant reception at the Academy of Sciences and another ovation at the theatre during a performance of *Alzire*, Voltaire set the Academy to work on a project into which he flung all his enthusiasm. It should undertake in earnest its Dictionary of the French Language, but on a new and scientific plan which he outlined. Voltaire died as the modern science of philology was beginning, but in his own somewhat empirical way this master of the craft of words had a profound respect for the language he had carried to perfection, and he saw the need for systematic study. He overbore the laziness of his brother academicians, and extorted from them a promise that each should undertake one letter of the alphabet: for his own part he would do A.

Voltaire was now, at 84, looking forward to a new lease of life in Paris, and he actually bought a house. His wiser friends and his doctors counselled in vain a prompt return to Ferney. Had they won, he might conceivably have lived long enough to see the Revolution—long enough, it may be, to be sentenced, like his disciple Condorcet, to the guillotine. What actually happened was that he wore himself out in writing, in great excitement, a memorandum for the Academy on the Dictionary. He sat up all night to complete it, drank incredible quantities of coffee, lost in consequence the ability to sleep, and was soon in a high fever. He then took an overdose of an opiate, which completed the ruin of his over-worked brain. His mind wandered: he could take no food, and for days on end he lay in silent torpor. He had, however, lucid intervals. During one of them he wrote a madrigal: in another he was made happy by the news of Lally's vindication. On May 30th his nephew, Abbé Mignot, sent for the parish priest and Father

Gaultier, and undertook that he would make an adequate retractation of all unorthodoxy. When the two priests arrived, Voltaire
failed to recognize the curé, but pressed Gaultier's hand affectionately. The curé insisted that he should explicitly recognize the
divinity of Jesus Christ. Voltaire sat up, made a gesture of im-
patience and said, 'Let me die in peace.' Thereupon the priests left
him to die in his sins.

The end came on this day. About his last hours clerical writers
have invented to the greater glory of God many tales, some childish,
some filthy, all doubtless edifying. The facts are placed beyond
doubt by the testimony of Belle et Bonne, who never quitted him.
'Up to the last moment everything breathed the benevolence and
goodness of his character. Everything bespoke in him tranquillity,
peace, resignation, save for the little movement of annoyance
against the curè of Saint-Sulpice, when he asked him to withdraw,
and said to him, "Let me die in peace." '

It remains to tell the story of this old man's bones. They became
the prize for which two irreconcilable armies contended. Voltaire
had humbled himself in vain: the Archbishop of Paris would allow
neither a regular burial in his diocese, nor the rite customary for all
academicians, a memorial service in the Church of the Cordeliers.
His nephew, however, was abbot of the monastery of Scellières,
and to it Voltaire's body was carried. The Bishop of Troyes issued
an interdict, but it arrived an hour too late to stop the burial in its
half-ruined chapel. The abbot was deposed for his share in this
irregular performance. The lodge of the Nine Sisters held a memorial
ceremony later in the year, and in Berlin Frederick caused a requiem
to be sung in the Catholic Cathedral.

Thirteen years passed, and at its height the Revolution recognized its intellectual father. His tragedy *Brutus* became its manifesto
on the stage, and every performance of it was a political demonstration. After one of them, as the house rang with cheers, Citizen
Villette, the husband of Belle et Bonne and once Marquis of this
name, rose and proposed that Voltaire's bones should be brought
back to Paris with revolutionary honours. The idea commended
itself to everyone, and a decree authorized the Society of Friends of
the Constitution to carry it out. On a stormy day in July, 1791, the

body was carried in state through the streets of the capital. In the procession walked the patriots who had just brought back the King a prisoner from Varennes. There were actors and actresses in Roman costume, contemporaries as it were of Brutus. With them were the workmen who had demolished the Bastille, carrying a model of that gloomy fortress that twice had counted Voltaire an inmate. On its liberated site the procession halted to do its prisoner honour. At its head walked the two daughters of Jean Calas, with Belle et Bonne, as chief mourners. The inscription on the bier ran thus: 'He avenged Calas, La Barre, Sirven and Montbailly. Poet, philosopher and historian, he gave a mighty impetus to the human mind: he made us ready for freedom.'

Beside Jean-Jacques Rousseau, the feud that divided them forgotten, the bones of Voltaire were laid within the classical structure of the church of Sainte-Geneviève, known henceforward as the Panthéon.[1] On its walls was graven the inscription: 'To great men the fatherland in gratitude.'

What shall we say of this extraordinary man? One statement about him, and possibly only one, is uncontentious. In this fragile dynamo, Nature concentrated an intellectual energy that would have sufficed to render a dozen men famous and useful in their several ways. No obstacle, no weight of authority intimidated him. He challenged, with an audacity that has few parallels in the records of our race, a power that had held civilization in bondage since the first measurement of time. With daring he united two gifts that it rarely commands, a patient and methodical industry and the graces of a sensitive art. He laboured incessantly through sixty years of maturity; and in all of the many contrasted tasks that his wide interests set him, he excelled. He could turn from the writing of a lucid treatise on physics to a madrigal that sings. He could compose with equal mastery a history that demanded sustained research and disciplined restraint, or a satire that succeeded by its headlong spontaneity. The man who was at home over the whole range of

[1] Until 1897 it was the belief of French anti-clericals, Voltaire's biographer Desnoiresterres among them, that at the Restoration pious hands with the consent of the Church robbed the vaults of the two bodies and flung them into a ditch. In that year, by the order of the Ministry of the day, the coffins were examined and found intact.

human history could adjust himself to the writing of a pamphlet on contemporary happenings, focused with perfect tact for minds that live in their day. Grave tragedies and gay little tales, reflective poems and stinging epigrams, familiar letters and sober histories— he handled all these forms with equal ease. He wielded language, the most human of all man's tools, with a skill and power that move opponents to envy and friends to a delight that never tires. In the exquisite control of words one asks whether any writer in any age has surpassed him. Courage, art, endurance, these were his.

So far there can be little difference of opinion. But conservative critics maintain that these rare powers were put to a detestable use, and of this they find the explanation in the frailties of Voltaire's character. It happens that posterity knows in minute detail all the evil this man did in his crowded life of eighty-four years. He practised no concealment. He confessed daily in his exuberant correspondence. He lived in a society that relished gossip and scandal. He had many vigilant enemies, among them that religious Order which turned espionage into a fine art. His few deplorable actions have been frankly told in these pages, but space failed to relate many of his good deeds—his generosity to struggling young poets, the delicate and anonymous help he gave to La Harpe and others. The blots are conspicuous enough. He lied with facility. He dodged and retreated with scant regard to dignity or honour. He was merciless to an insignificant scribbler who sought gain by slandering him. In making money, he followed the usual practices of the shrewd man of business. It was not a scrupulous society in which he was reared by the least scrupulous branch of a corrupt Church. Then shall we weigh his ill deeds against the good? That is the morality of the nursery. This man, compact of great virtues and frailties, was a single organism. The good and the evil in him sprang from the same root. The secret of his power was a certain intensity of concentration, an ability to direct all his energies into one channel at a time. If he gave way to anger, he would be merciless. If his sympathies were roused, he would put all else aside, through years of sustained effort, to succour a fellow-citizen in distress. At a summons to action, all of him went instantly to limbs, or tongue or pen. Once at a rehearsal, he was inciting an actress to swifter physical movement. 'To do what you want,' she answered, 'I should have to have a devil in my body.' 'That's it,' answered Voltaire, 'to have a devil in one's body is the secret of success in all the arts.' This dæmonic abandonment was the essence of the man. It caused him to rush straight to his goal, instinctively, with the minimum of reflection or self-criticism. Of such a man it is proper to ask but one question: What was his goal?

Who would hesitate, after reading his writings and scanning his life, to name his goal? 'God and Liberty' was the last motto in which he summed it up for himself. Certainly from the hour that the doors of the Bastille slammed upon him, down to his joy on his death-bed over the erasure of Lally's sentence, he worked for liberty. He sought to break the fetters that Church and King had laid upon the human intellect. He laboured to make a humane and impersonal law supreme above a despot's will. But this is too slight as a statement of his goal. He sought above all else to erect for society a new scheme of values among the goods that men desire. He found it in the exaltation of constructive work for the common good. He smashed the barriers of nationality and creed, that in this effort separate mankind. He saw, across wars and schisms, the great cosmopolitan society. He preached, as the one sufficient commandment, the love of one's fellowmen, and made it concrete and vital, by his relentless assaults upon every form of cruelty. 'Words,' do you say? Yes, he had words for all this, so strong, so witty, that some of them have passed into the daily speech even of other nations. But the peasants of his mountains, the children of Calas, the horses that drew his plough knew that his words were sincere.

This, then, was the goal that the owner of these unrivalled talents sought. How many saints in the Church's calendar have a record of service to man that will compare with his? His friends knew him. Here is the verdict of the ablest intellect and the finest character among them. 'If virtue,' wrote Condorcet, 'consists in doing good and in loving mankind with passion, what man has had more virtue?'

BIBLIOGRAPHY

The first important edition of Voltaire's works, edited by Beaumarchais and Condorcet, runs to 70 volumes (Kehl 1784–89). It includes Condorcet's *Life*. The best, though inadequate, edition is that by Moland in 54 vols. (1877–83). A critical edition by Theodore Besterman of the *Correspondence* is in progress at the Institut and Musée Voltaire, Geneva, and will run to 20,000 letters in nearly 100 volumes. He has also published Voltaire's *Notebooks* (1952). Some individual works (but not the most important) are available in critical and popular editions. The usual selections from his poems and letters are marred by the omission of anything likely to offend good Roman Catholics.

The standard life by Gustave Desnoiresterres, in 8 stout volumes, is honest, and readable in spite of its bulk. Unfortunately it is now quite out of date so far as Voltaire's ideas are concerned, these having since been discussed in a very large number of works such as *Voltaire's politics*, by Peter Gay (Princeton 1959) and *La Religion de Voltaire*, by René Pomeau (Nizet 1956).

Of small biographies in French by far the best is *Voltaire*, by Gustave Lanson. Michelet's *History of France* should be consulted, and *Le XVIIIe Siècle*, by E. Faguet.

Two contemporary translations of Voltaire's Works appeared in England; the first under Smollett's nominal editorship in 35 volumes (1761–74), and the second edited by William Kenrick in 1779–81. These collections contain much that few modern readers want, but omit some of Voltaire's best work. They contain, however, the histories, the Dictionary, and most of the tales, but very few letters. Messrs. Harpers' *The Best Known Works of Voltaire* (1932) includes *Candide*. The Broadway Translations (Routledge) include *Zadig and other Tales* and Voltaire's *Correspondence with Frederick the Great*. Translations of *Charles XII* and the *Century of Louis XIV* are in Everyman's Library. Selections from the *Philosophic Dictionary* have been translated by H. I. Woolf (Allen & Unwin, 1924). The only good selection from the letters, *Select Letters*, is by Besterman (Nelson 1962).

By far the best Life in English is by S. G. Tallentyre (2 volumes, 1903). *Voltaire*, by C. E. Vulliamy (1930), is an entertaining biography enriched by full translations from the letters. *Voltaire*, by Richard Aldington (1925), contains a valuable guide to his writings.

Of monographs in English the most notable are by John Morley and J. M. Robertson. The former is marred by its Victorian puritanism: *Candide* with all the tales is thought worthy of exactly a third of a page. Essays by Carlyle and Lytton Strachey (*Books and Characters*) should be noted. There is much in Carlyle's *Frederick* and in Macaulay's *Essays*.

Among more general books may be mentioned Lecky's *History of Rationalism* and Kingsley Martin's *French Liberal Thought in the Eighteenth Century*. Consult *The Huguenots*, by A. J. Grant; *Political Thought in England from Locke to Bentham*, by Harold Laski; and *A History of the Freedom of Thought 600 B.C.—A.D. 1912*, by J. B. Bury.

The standard bibliography is by G. Bengesco in 4 volumes, indexes and supplements to which have recently been published. In general, the Voltaire Institute's series of *Studies on Voltaire and the Eighteenth Century* is indispensable.

INDEX

Academy, French, 30
Adam, Father, 103
Adrian IV, 56
Alexander III, 56, 67
Alfred the Great, 61, 67
Alzire, 17, 131
Anabaptists, 69
Angell, Sir Norman, 73
Annals of the Empire, The, 54, 81
Arouet, Armand, 8, 10
Arouet Family, 8, 17
Augustine, St., 9

Babouc: or, The Way of the World, 90
Bacon, 67
Barre, de la, 108–9
Bartholomew, Massacre of St., 19
Bastille: first imprisonment, 14
    second imprisonment, 20
Beauregard, de, 130
Belle et Bonne. See Villette, Marquise de
Benedict XIV, 42
Bolingbroke, 18, 22
Bossuet, 47, 50
Boswell, 102
Boyer, Bishop, 41
Brahe, Tycho, 67
Brutus, 24, 37, 132
Buckle, 47
Buffon, 58, 129
Burke, 49
Byng, Admiral, 109–10
Byron, 40

Calas, Jean, 104, 106, 108
Candide, 56, 57, 85, 90, 96
Carlyle, 49
Catherine II, 54, 98, 102
Caumartin, de, 12
Charlemagne, 66
Charles XII, History of, 25, 32, 35, 49, 51, 54, 72
Charles XII, 52, 53
Châtelet, Marquise de, 34, 36, 38–39, 43, 45, 50, 78, 83
Châtelet, Marquis de, 34, 36
Châteauneuf, Abbé de, 8, 13
Châteauneuf, Marquis de, 11

Clarke, Samuel, 23
Colbert, 67, 68
Comte, 68
Condorcet, Marquis de, 31, 47, 59, 64, 71, 125, 131, 135
Congreve, 24
Constantine, 66
Corneille, 8, 14, 15, 16, 85
Customs. See *Essay*

D'Alembert, 40, 71, 99, 111, 129, 130
Dangeville, Mlle, 37
Daniel, 50
d'Argental, 32, 37, 126
d'Argens, 76
Darwin, 58
Dauphin, 42
Defoe, 53
d'Ennery, 67
Denis, Madame, 75, 80, 102, 126
Descartes, 31
Desfontaine, 43
Diatribe of Dr. Akakia, The, 80, 81
Diderot, 37, 60, 99, 101
Dryden, 17, 20
Dunoyer, Madame Olympe, 11–12

Edward III, 72
Emerson, 57
Essay on Customs, 38, 51, 54, 55, 56, 57, 65, 116, 118
Étallonde, 108

Falkener, Sir Everard, 23
Fashion, The Man of, 39
Fleury, Cardinal, 26, 32, 41, 42
Fontenelle, 129
Franklin, Benjamin, 126
Frederick the Great, 38, 40, 41, 45, 50, 75, 76, 77, 80
Fréron, 43

Gaultier, Father, 127, 132
Gay, 22, 23
George I, 22, 24
George II, 24
Gibbon, 48
Godwin, 59, 64

Goethe, 17, 38
Gortz, Baron, 53

Helvétius, 37, 59
Henriade, 14, 18, 25
Henri IV, 19, 67
Henry the Navigator, 62
Hirsch, 77
History of Scarmentado's Travels, The, 90
Hobbes, 58
Hume, David, 48, 101

Irène, 125, 129

Jansenism, 9–10, 56, 83
Jesuits, 9, 10–11, 54, 56
Johnson, Samuel, 23, 51
Julius II, 72

Kaiserling, Baron, 38
Kant, 122
Kepler, 67
König, Professor, 78

La Beaumelle, 43
La Harpe, 102
La Mettrie, 77
Lally, Count, 110
Lecouvreur, Mlle, 19, 31
Leibnitz, 33, 78, 82, 83
Lenclos, Ninon de, 8
Lessing, 16
Letters on England, 65, 68
L'Ingénu, 90, 91
Locke, 27, 30, 31, 114
Lorraine, Duke of, 45
Louis XI, 67, 68
Louis XIV, 10, 13, 52, 66, 67, 69, 73, 74
Louis XIV, Century of, 40, 48, 51, 52, 53–54, 56, 62, 70, 118
Louis XV, 20, 42, 49, 52, 75, 96, 125
Louis XVI, 125, 129

Mahomed, 17, 38, 42, 97
Mahomed II, 72
Maid, The, 39, 40, 76
Maine, Duchess of, 44
Maintenon, Madame de, 52
Man with Forty Crowns, The, 97
Marie Antoinette, 129
Marlborough, Duchess of, 24, 53
Marx, Karl, 47
Maupertuis, 60, 77, 78, 79
Mazarin, 67
Mérope, 16, 17, 38, 41

Micromegas, 90, 91
Mignot, Madame de, 10, 22
Mignot, Abbé, 131
Mill, 114
Milton, 57
Moisnel, 108
Molière, 9
Montbailly, Madame, 109
Montesquieu, 25, 47, 48, 60, 92, 129
Morley, John, 40

Natural Law, 85, 123
Newton, Sir Isaac, 23, 26, 30, 31, 32, 34, 61

Œdipe, 14, 16, 17, 31
Oldfield, Anne, 32

Parlement of Paris, History of, 54
Parnell, Thomas, 44
Pascal, 9, 56, 84
Peter the Great, 49
Peter the Great, History of, 53, 54
Philip of Orleans. See Regent
Philosophic Dictionary, 64, 65, 69, 83, 85, 114, 115, 123
Philosophical Letters, 26, 32
Pimpette. See Dunoyer, Olympe
Pitt, Andrew, 23
Pompadour, Madame de, 44
Pope, 22, 23, 30, 33, 82
Port Royal, 10
Preliminary Remarks on the Thoughts of M. Pascal, 83
Princess of Babylon, The, 74, 90, 125
Prodigal Son, The, 44
Pucelle, La. See *Maid, The*

Quakers, 23, 27

Rabelais, 95
Racine, 67, 85
Rameau, 35, 42
Regent (Philip of Orleans), 13, 14, 18
Richardson, 92, 95
Richelieu, Duke of, 8, 34, 66, 67, 110, 126
Rohan, Chevalier de, 19, 22
Rousseau, J.-B., 18, 32
Rousseau, J.-J., 25, 74, 85, 95, 100, 133
Rupelmonde, Madame de, 18

Saint-Cyran, M. de, 9
Saint-Lambert, Marquis de, 45
Saint-Pierre, Abbé de, 74
Saladin, 72

Sermon of the Fifty, The, 100
Shakespeare, 16, 30, 35
Sirven, 108
Spengler, Oswald, 90
Stanislas of Poland, King, 45, 53
Sterne, 92
Sully, Duke of, 8, 14, 20, 67
Swift, Dean, 22, 23, 92

Tacitus, 75
Tamerlane, 72
Tancred, 17
Tellier, Le, 10
Temple, 13, 26, 33
Temple of Glory, The, 42
Temple of Taste, The, 32
Thiériot, 12, 24, 25
Tolstoy, 15, 95
Travenol, 43
Treatise on Metaphysics, 121
Treatise on Tolerance, 112
Tsarina Catherine, 50, 60
Turgot, 67, 71, 98, 126

Unitarians, 27, 128
Urania, Epistle to, 32

Varicourt, Mlle de, 103

Vico, 47
Villette, Marquis de, 103, 132
Villette, Marquise de, 125, 132
Voltaire:
   physique and temperament, 7–8
   as a youth, 12–13
   as amateur actor, 15–16
   influence of England on, 25–26
   as philosopher, 33
   music, 35
   habits of work, 36
   courtesy, 37
   scientific studies, 38
   study and writing of history, 47
   moralist of genius, 49
   aloofness to religious thought, 56–57

War of Geneva, The, 101
Wells, H. G., 49
Wicliffe, 61
William of Orange, 29, 67, 72
Wordsworth, 94

Young, 24

Zadig, 44, 90
Zaire, 31, 32

Printed by
Cox & Wyman Ltd,
London, Fakenham and Reading

478